the *Casual* Naturalist's GUIDE to the Salish Sea

Gary Schaan and Nancy Dolan

CasualNaturalist Press
Victoria British Columbia Canada

Canadian cataloguing in Publication Data

> Dolan, Nancy, 1949-
>   The CasualNaturalist's Guide to the Salish Sea
> Schaan, Gary, 1950-
>   The CasualNaturalist's Guide to the Salish Sea
> ISBN 0-9685708-0-1
> 1. Natural history - British Columbia - Washington State
> 2. Guidebook - Ferries - Roads
>   I. Title

Published by CasualNaturalist Press
P.O. Box 5773
Victoria, BC Canada V8R 6S8
E-mail casualnaturalist@home.com
www.casualnaturalist.com

Printed in Canada
by Friesen Printers, Altona, Manitoba

Research and writing by Gary Schaan
Design and production by Nancy Dolan

Contents

Acknowledgements

The authors are most grateful to

Marie O'Shaughnessy
Derrick Ditchburn
Philip Critchlow
and
Jonathan Grant
for access to their photo collections.

We also express our thanks to

Ray Bigauskas, Anne Delves,
Kathleen Elliot and Marie O'Shaughnessy
for editing and proofing
and
Beverly van Druten-Blais
for production pre-flighting
the manuscript.

Introduction

The southwestern corner of Canada and the adjoining northwestern tip of the United States form a single ecosystem containing an exceptional variety of marine and terrestrial habitats – from open ocean and island-dotted sounds to temperate rainforests and glacier-covered mountains. This is one of the most biologically productive regions on earth with some of the top birding, whale watching and tidepooling sites in the Americas.

The Casual**Naturalist's Guide** describes trips to many of the best and most scenic wildlife habitats in the Salish Sea. It is intended for travellers of all ages and abilities who want to comfortably explore the region and have from a few days to a few weeks to do so. Along with overviews of the region's natural history, the Guide includes maps and  directions for 25 ferry and road routes, each accompanied by descriptions and illustrative photos. Additional information on over 75 different recommended sites is conveniently organized by characteristic habitats found along each route.

The name **Salish Sea** derives from the language of the original peoples inhabiting this region. The First Nations had an intimate knowledge of sustainable use of the region's natural riches. Their tradition of ownership over the lands and waters is still suggested by place names taken from the Salish language.

Using the Guide

The Guide contains maps and descriptions for 5 ferry routes and 20 road routes, with information on what the traveller can expect to see. Each route *(see the index on Page 48)* is also identified on the overview map on Page 49. The routes are grouped and colour coded according to the types of wildlife habitats they represent. This will help you plan your trip, as well as suggest natural history features along the way. Each road route also includes directions and details on recommended stops, while the wildlife symbols indicate what you might expect to see at each of these sites. Interpretive centres are also indicated.

Measurements are given in metric and American units as follows:

- km/miles is kilometres/miles
- m/ft is metres/feet
- cm/inches is centimetres/inches
- C/F is Centigrade/Fahrenheit

The common names used for animals and plants were selected from local usages.

At the back of the Guide are telephone numbers, addresses and web sites for ferry operators; national, provincial and state parks; and government tourism offices.

black-capped chickadee

Wildlife Cautions

There are cougars and black bears in the forests and mountains around the Salish Sea. As rewarding as it is to catch a glimpse of these animals, they are powerful carnivores and potentially dangerous. Avoid feeding or approaching these animals, as well as deer and other wildlife. This is for their benefit as much as for yours.

Cougars tend to be active at night and secretive. Their main prey are black-tailed deer. Attacks on humans occur infrequently. If there are signs of cougar, keep small children and pets at hand. While generally elusive, every fall a number of cougars wander into Victoria. They are tranquillized, captured and then released in more isolated areas.

Black bears are extremely fast and powerful animals. If you see signs such as scats *(bear droppings)* indicating that bears are in the area, make noises when walking through bush or forest. This will warn the bear and help avoid an unpleasant surprise. Bears should never be approached or fed. If you encounter a bear, remain calm; do not provoke it; slowly move away. Food and garbage should always be stored in sealed containers as bears have a very acute sense of smell.

Wildlife Viewing

The waters and adjoining lands of the Salish Sea offer an abundance of sites to view wildlife, wildflowers or the magnificent temperate rainforests. The Wildlife Symbols found throughout the Guide indicate what you can reasonably expect to see at any of the described sites. Remember that viewing possibilities vary with the season, as well as with the time of day and the weather.

 whales and dolphins

 other marine mammals

 deer, bears and other large mammals

 eagles, hawks and vultures

 shore and wading birds

 seabirds and waterfowl

 songbirds and upland birds

 intertidal life

 salmon runs

 forests or trees of special interest

 exceptional wildflower viewing

 interpretive centre

Victoria shoreline

sunrise at Witty's Lagoon

winter scene at Spectacle Lake

Light on Prevost Island

Landscape, Climate & Geology

Landscape, climate and geological history have all combined to influence the development of the Salish Sea's ecosystem with its diversity of marine, coastal and terrestrial habitats.

Sea

Centred on the San Juan Islands, the Salish Sea encompasses three long arms. The Strait of Juan de Fuca extends west 150 km/95 miles to the Pacific Ocean. The Strait of Georgia ends 230 km/145 miles north at Campbell River where it merges into Johnstone Strait. Puget Sound runs south 180 km/115 miles to Olympia. The average depth of this inland sea is 155 m/510 ft.

Mountains

The region has four distinct mountain ranges. The Vancouver Island Ranges and the Olympic Mountains are the most westerly. Separated by the Strait of Juan de Fuca, they both rise from narrow coastal plains bordering the Pacific Ocean. The highest peak in the Vancouver Island Ranges is Golden Hinde (2,200 m/7,260 ft). In the Olympic Mountains, Mount Olympus rises to 2,414 m/7,965 ft.

The Coast Mountains north of Vancouver and the Cascade Mountains of Washington State form the eastern border of the region. These granitic mountains include numerous peaks and ridges from 2,100 to 2,700 m/7,000 to 9,000 ft. The Cascades include Mt. Baker, 75 km/45 miles east of the San Juan Islands. For many residents on both sides of the border this beautiful snow-clad dormant volcano symbolizes the Salish Sea. Mt. Rainier, the area's highest peak at 4,392 m/14,410 ft, marks the southern reaches of the region.

Climate

The overriding influence affecting the marine, coastal and terrestrial habitats found in the Salish Sea is the abundance of fresh water found as rain, in rivers, or in mountain snowpacks.

The cool ice-free waters of the North Pacific Ocean result in a moderate climate. There are two distinct seasons, both with mild temperatures - a sunny dry summer and an overcast wet winter. Running north to south, the mountain chains protect the region from both the continental climate to the east and the strong storms and winds of the North Pacific to the west. Except in the mountains, there is a long frost-free growing

season. In inland locales, summer temperatures tend to be higher than on the coast, and winter temperatures, lower. Valleys, peaks and long indented coastlines create numerous microclimates.

The long mild spring begins in March as the North Pacific High weather pattern forms offshore. Coastal areas become frost-free during April, or further inland in May. Summers are the dry season when westerly winds prevail. Maximum temperatures are reached in July and August, with average lows around 10C/50F and highs around 20C/70F.

Offshore in October, the Alaska Low replaces the North Pacific High bringing intense stormfronts of rain and clouds. Gales and high seas batter the inner coasts. Frost occurs by November at low elevations inland and by December on the coasts. Average January lows are 2C/36F with highs averaging 6C/43F.

Climate

hyper maritime outer coast

The most spectacular rainforests are found in the west-facing valleys of the outer coasts which receive 300-380 cm/120-150 inches of rain a year. Even in summer, the coastal plains receive moisture from sea fog. In winter, intense deluges of rain take place. Ucluelet, on the west coast of Vancouver Island, has recorded 49 cm/19 inches of rain in one winter day.

snowy mountains

Massive amounts of precipitation combine with alpine temperatures to create awesome snowfalls and the most southerly glaciers on the North Pacific Coast. The upper slopes of the Olympic Mountains average 500 cm/200 inches of precipitation annually. Typical subalpine snowpack is 3 m/10 ft, while 13 m/40 ft of winter snow fall is common at elevations over 1,500 m/5,000 ft. In the winter of 1998/99 so much snow fell that ski resorts on Vancouver Island stopped measuring the ski base at 10 m/33 ft when they had to dig out the chairlifts. The same winter 29 m/95 ft of snow fell on Mt. Baker.

rainshadow

Protected by the Olympic Mountains from westerly winds, Port Townsend, Victoria, and the San Juan and southern Gulf Islands share a distinct sunny and mild climate with a long frost-free growing season. Sequim, only 50 km/30 miles to the east of wet Mt. Olympus, receives only 44 cm/17 inches of rain. Victoria, which averages 68 cm/27 inches of rain, is one of the sunniest locations in Canada. These locations often share a sunny and cloudless sky surrounded in all directions by massive cloud formations.

maritime inner coast

The lowlands bordering Puget Sound, the northern Strait of Georgia and the Fraser Valley, including the cities of Vancouver and Seattle, receive rainfall in the range of 80-120 cm/32-48 inches. Temperatures become less moderate eastward up the inland valleys, while rainfall increases with proximity to mountains. In winter, cold arctic outflows move westward down valleys and fiords bringing sub-zero temperatures and snow to the coast.

Fire and Ice

Victoria is one of the finest locations for viewing the complex geological history of the Salish Sea. On a clear day the majestic volcanic cone of Mt. Baker rises to the east over the San Juan Islands. To the south are the snow-capped sedimentary rocks of the Olympic Mountains rising above the white bluffs of glacially deposited silt which form the Olympic shoreline. The exposed rock in and around Victoria shows the effect of geological forces such as plate tectonics, volcanic activity, glaciation and erosion from waves and rain. Smooth pillow basalts were formed from undersea volcanoes; limestones, from ancient reefs; and sandstone deposits, from eroding mountains. Polished and grooved rock formations, and gravel and sand beds are the result of retreating ice sheets.

Fire and Ice

fire

The northwest coast of North America developed intermittently over hundreds of millions of years through additions from continental drift, by the uplifting and erosion of mountains and through volcanic activity. Vancouver Island originated in tropical latitudes as the Wrangellia Terrane, an arc of islands which drifted

north to collide 100 million years ago with the ancient uplands of the Coast and Cascade Mountains. Periods of mountain building caused by the buckling of colliding continental

ice scoured gneiss

plates, volcanic activity and lava deposits alternated with periods of erosion. Offshore, 200 km/125 miles west of Tofino, the spreading ocean floor is still pushing the Juan de Fuca Plate under the North America Plate. At depths of 150-200 km/80-125 miles, the subducted plate melts and magma rises to form a volcanic arc which extends 1,000 km/650 miles from Northern California through Washington State into British Columbia. It is now understood that catastrophic earthquakes occur every 300-900 years when the strain of the compression of the two plates against each other is released.

ice

Fourteen thousand years ago, glaciers from the Vancouver Island Ranges, and the Olympic, Coast and Cascade Mountains converged to form the Cordilleran Ice Sheet. Ice scoured out sediments in Puget Sound, the Strait of Georgia and the Strait of Juan de Fuca, leaving U shaped valleys and fiords. When the ice retreated 10,000 years ago, ocean waters inundated the coastal plains. At that time Victoria's present day shoreline was under 90 m/295 ft of water. It took 5,000 years for the depressed land to rebound from the weight of the 1.5 km/1 mile thick ice sheet.

Geologic Timeline

years ago	the first million years
50	magnitude 7.3 earthquake on Vancouver Island
120	last eruption of Mt. Baker
300	magnitude 9 earthquake
500	Mt. Rainier mudflow buries Puyallup Valley
1,100	earthquake lifts Bainbridge Island 7 m/23 ft
5,000	present shoreline rebounds 60-120 m/200-400 ft from weight of glaciers
10,000	ocean floods in as glacial ice leaves lowlands
14,000	glaciation stops at Olympia
20,000	Mt. Garibaldi forms under 2 km/1.25 miles of glacial ice
29,000	Fraser Glacial Period begins
500,000	Mt. Rainier forms
1,000,000	Georgia Basin/Puget Trough form and fill with sediment.

millions of years ago	the geologic foundation
5	Cascade volcanic arc created
20	subduction of Juan de Fuca Plate uplifts mountains on Olympic Peninsula and Vancouver Island
35 to 40	accretions of terranes form Olympics and modify southern Vancouver Island
100	Vancouver Island (Wrangellia Terrane) collides with North America uplifting Coast and Cascade Mountains
130	granite rocks of Coast and Cascade Mountains adhere to the edge of North America
155 to 380	Wrangellia Terrane forms as tropical islands – layers of volcanic and coral reef deposits

A Mixing of Waters

The biological riches of the Salish Sea are a result of daily and seasonal mixing of waters. Massive tidal rivers flow in and out of the Strait of Juan de Fuca past thousands of rocks and islands. You can observe the effects in the tidal rips, whirlpools and large standing waves seen off the Victoria shoreline, at Admiralty Inlet, in Active Pass and at other sites. The turbulence mixes cold, salty ocean waters with brackish surface waters.

Trial Island & Olympic Mountains

Tides range from 2.5 m/8 ft around the San Juan Islands, to 3.4 m/11 ft near Texada Island and as high as 4.6 m/15 ft at Olympia. It takes from several months to a year for deeper waters of the Salish Sea to be exchanged with waters from the Pacific. Average water temperatures in the Strait of Juan de Fuca are 6C/43F in winter and 12C/54F in summer. Summer water temperatures in the Strait of Georgia average 15C/59F, but are often warmer in the sheltered bays found in the Strait and in Puget Sound.

In June and July melting mountain snowpacks load the many rivers with silt - a rich nutrient for life in the Salish Sea. You can see this phenomenon from the Vancouver - Victoria ferry at Active Pass as a dramatic change in water colour from mud brown to azure blue. The Fraser River water is stained brown by countless microscopic living diatoms fertilized by river nutrients. This river drains 200,000 square kilometres/75,000 square miles of mountains and valleys in British Columbia, providing 80% of the fresh water flowing into the Salish Sea, and depositing 20,000,000 tons of silt annually in the Fraser Delta. Compare the river's peak flow of 10-15,000 cubic m per second in June, to a trickle of 700 cubic m per second in winter when most of the moisture is stored in snowpacks.

Introduction to the Ferry Routes

Take full advantage of the many ferries which crisscross the Salish Sea to see the region's spectacular scenery: deep rocky fiords, kelp beds, tree covered islands, oyster farms in sheltered bays and snow-capped volcanoes. The ferries are appreciated by visitors and residents alike as a relaxing and inexpensive way to observe marine birds and mammals.

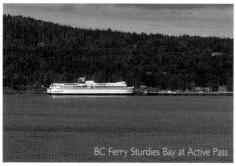
BC Ferry Sturdies Bay at Active Pass

Both BC Ferries and Washington State Ferries operate as extensions of the highway systems. Crossing times vary from 15 minutes to 4 hours. There are also privately operated car and passenger-only ferries. Schedules can be obtained through the telephone numbers provided in the Trip Planning section at the back of the Guide. Reservations are available on some routes.

Gulf Island Ferry

Using the Maps and Descriptions

The Guide describes five of the most interesting ferry passages in the Salish Sea. Detailed maps and accompanying text will assist you in locating and identifying features of interest. In using the maps and descriptions of the ferry routes, note the following symbols:

 Wildlife symbols indicate viewing opportunities

 indicates the location on the map corresponding to the narrative

 Look for a lighthouse.

 Look for a mountain or large hill.

 Look for a ferry terminal.

At the end of this section are three other ferry route maps showing the many sailings operated by BC Ferries and Washington State Ferries. In the section on road routes you will also find descriptions of several of the shorter ferry crossings.

Marine Habitat

From the ferries you will often see rafts of seabirds feeding in open waters. These birds are evidence of the rich marine habitats hidden below the surface. The Salish Sea is home to 200 species of fish, 500 marine invertebrates, 135 marine birds and 26 marine mammals, all sustained directly or indirectly by the bountiful plankton found in these waters.

Spring brings growth in the sea as well as on land. Increased sunlight and a nutrient-rich broth of river sediments support a

common murre

remarkable growth of algae and other microscopic plants (*phytoplankton*). By April or May, the sea turns a semi-opaque green. Microscopic animals floating in the water (*zooplankton*) feed on the phytoplankton, and in turn become food for shrimp and small fish. One of these fish, the Pacific herring, is found in remarkable abundance. It forms the main part of the diet of many seabirds including the harlequin duck and cormorants, as well as seals and fish such as salmon and lingcod. Then in June, the algae bloom subsides. One final small bloom takes place in late summer before the waters clear in fall and winter, making these the preferred seasons for scuba diving, in spite of the often adverse weather.

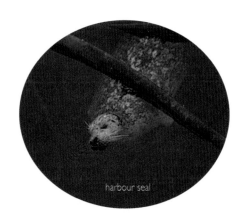
harbour seal

Marine Habitat

Fishing boats and orca whales indicate the presence of migrating schools of salmon. Sea lions feed on the rockfish and octopuses which live in the submerged reefs. Rockfish, living to 100 years, account for more species than any other family of fish in the Salish Sea. The giant Pacific octopus, weighing up to 45 kg/ 100 lbs with tentacles spreading to 5 m/16 ft, is also a reef dweller. Other fish feed upon the clams, worms, and crabs found on muddy bottoms. The Pacific halibut, a bottom feeder and a favoured catch of both commercial and sport fishermen, might weigh more than 100 kilograms/220 pounds.

salmon troller

red rockfish

Underwater rock walls found at sites with strong currents, such as Race Rocks or Quadra Island, rival tropical reefs in the amount and colour of life. Every square inch of rock is covered in growth – sponges, soft corals, anemones and other plants and animals. Jacques Cousteau, diving in these waters in the 1970's, declared them to be among the richest and best dive sites in the world. It is no wonder that the international environmental movement sprung from this area.

Pacific herring

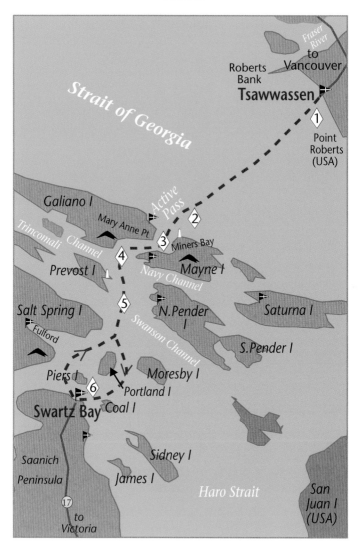

Strait of Georgia

Fraser River

to Vancouver

Roberts Bank

Tsawwassen

Point Roberts (USA)

Galiano I

Active Pass

Mary Anne Pt

Trincomali Channel

Miners Bay

Navy Channel

Prevost I

Mayne I

Salt Spring I

N.Pender I

Swanson Channel

Saturna I

Fulford

S.Pender I

Piers I

Moresby I

Portland I

Swartz Bay Coal I

Sidney I

Saanich Peninsula

James I

Haro Strait

San Juan I (USA)

to Victoria

Distance	44 km/28 miles
Crossing Time	1 hour 35 minutes
Operator	BC Ferries

Georgina Point

22

Stay on deck to see the snowcapped Coast Mountains and Vancouver Island Ranges as you weave through the Gulf Islands among sandstone cliffs, forests of Douglas-fir and madrone (arbutus), wildflower meadows and island retreats. Don't miss bald eagles, seals, and possibly orcas or other whales, in the tide rips and whirlpools of Active Pass.

BC Ferry

from **Tsawwassen**

① **N** of ferry terminal you will see Roberts Bank Superport and the Fraser River Delta. Look for great blue herons, willets and sandpipers feeding at the mudflats along the ferry causeway. **E** Nearby is Point Roberts (USA). **W** In the distance are the Gulf Islands.

② At the east entrance to Active Pass cormorants, terns, gulls and murrelets feed in tidal rips. In summer, note the change of water colour from the brown of the Fraser River to blue-green saltwater. **SE** is Georgina Point Lighthouse (1885) on Mayne Island. **E** is Mt. Baker.

③ Watch for orcas in summer in Miners Bay. **N** Bald eagles nest above the sandstone cliffs of Mary Anne Point. Ferries passing here present a wonderful photo opportunity.

④ The west entrance to Active Pass has 8 knot currents, tidal rips, seals and birds *(murres, scoters and loons)*. **E** Look for kelp beds at Helen Point on Mayne Island where Mt. Parke ▲ rises above Village Bay ⚑. **S** Kelp beds surround Enterprise Reef. **N** Collinson Point is below Mt. Galiano and Mt. Sutil ▲ on Galiano Island.

⑤ **W** Prevost Island sits in front of Saltspring Island. **E** Otter Bay ⚑ is on North Pender Island. **SE** Look for porpoises in Swanson Channel.

⑥ From the terminal, the ferry weaves among small islands, rocks and shoals to the north of Portland Island. Look for cormorants, crows and loons. **W** Mount Tuam ▲ and Fulford Harbour ⚑ are on Saltspring Island.

from **Swartz Bay**

For Gulf Islands ferry routes, see Page 38.

Victoria - Port Angeles

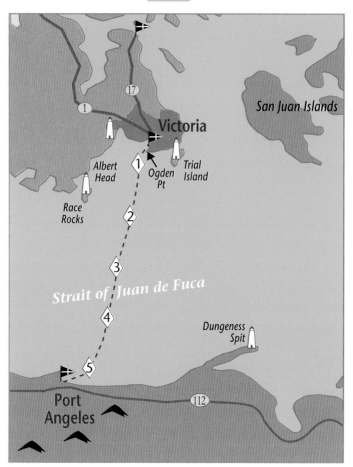

San Juan Islands

Victoria

Albert
Head

① Ogden
Pt

Trial
Island

Race
Rocks

②

③

Strait of Juan de Fuca

④

Dungeness
Spit

⑤

Port
Angeles

Distance	40 km/25 miles
Crossing Time	85 minutes, MV Coho *(car ferry)*
	60 minutes, Victoria Express *(passenger only)*
Operator	Black Ball Transport *(MV Coho)*
	Victoria Rapid Transit *(Victoria Express)*

cormorants

The Strait of Juan de Fuca has the feel of the open ocean with chances to see porpoises, gray or orca whales and ocean birds. Splendid views of the young

Coho ferry entering Victoria

mountains of the Olympic Peninsula contrast with the glacier scoured rocks of southern Vancouver Island.

from **Victoria**

① At the end of Victoria's Inner Harbour is the Empress Hotel. As you sail past the Ogden Point breakwater, look for kelp beds, seals, sea lions, great blue herons, bald eagles, gulls and cormorants. **W** Historic Fort Rodd Hill and lighthouse ⌂ guard the home of Canada's Pacific Fleet. **NE** Trial Island ⌂ lines up with distant Mt. Baker.

② **W** On clear days you can observe distant Race Rocks Lighthouse ⌂ built of 4 foot thick granite in 1860. The island is now an ecological preserve. Watch for Dall's porpoises following the ship. Occasionally orcas move through.

③ **W** At mid-strait notice the swell of waves from the Pacific Ocean. Summer fog might be encountered even in good weather. You might see pelagic *(open ocean)* birds – soaring shearwaters and petrels. On the water, common murres and ancient murrelets appear incongruously small.

Fisgard Lighthouse

④ **S** Port Angeles is flanked on the east by Blue Mountain, Mt. Tyler and Mt. Baldy ⏶. **W**est of the smokestacks are Mt. Angeles ⏶ and the deep cut Elwha River valley.
SE Dungeness Spit National Wildlife Refuge ⌂ is framed by the white bluffs of glacial deposits along the shore.

⑤ Port Angeles harbour has California sea lions, harbour seals, cormorants, loons and other birds. As the ferry rounds the end of Ediz Hook sandspit and the Coast Guard station, notice the kelp beds which shelter herring and salmon.

from **Port Angeles**

Giant Kelp

bull kelp

From a ferry or the shore you might notice forests of bull kelp fringing the rocky reefs and coasts. Examine kelp close up on a beach where it washes ashore after a storm. This brown algae can grow 20 m/66 ft in one season. What seems to be a root is actually the holdfast which attaches to rocks. The long, hollow, thin stem and the floats support the fronds. Like trees in a forest, kelp creates a habitat sheltering many species of fish and invertebrates. It also protects the shoreline from erosion.

sea urchin

Urchins, which graze on algae including kelp, are a favourite food for the sea otter. When fur hunters killed all the sea otters on the west coast of Vancouver Island in the 1800's, waves began eroding beaches fronting ancient Native villages on Barkley Sound as the urchins destroyed the kelp beds. The reintroduction of the otter should allow coastal habitats to recover.

Giant Kelp

pacific scallops

bull kelp

greater yellowlegs

lichen on rocky shore

sea lion rocks

Anacortes to Sidney
(San Juan Islands)

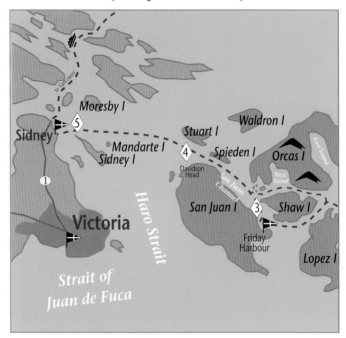

Distance	69 km/43 miles
Crossing Time	Approx. 3 hours
Operator	Washington State Ferries

The scenery and abundant marine life seen from this ferry will keep you on deck throughout the trip. In the rainshadow of the Olympic Mountains and Vancouver Island are 450 islands and rocks cloaked with Douglas-fir and madrone trees, and spring wildflowers on moss-covered slopes and in grass clearings. In Rosario Strait, a superb environment for marine birds, cormorants and black oystercatchers breed on Bird Rocks. Haro Strait has orcas, and Mandarte Island is a breeding site for tufted puffins, cormorants and gulls. Watch for porpoises, seals, bald and golden eagles, turkey vultures and tufted puffins on this route.

from **Anacortes**

① **N** of Anacortes ferry terminal are Cypress and Guemes Islands. Look for Mt. Baker to the east. On the water are scoters, terns and gulls; orca and Minke whales; and Dall's and harbour porpoises.

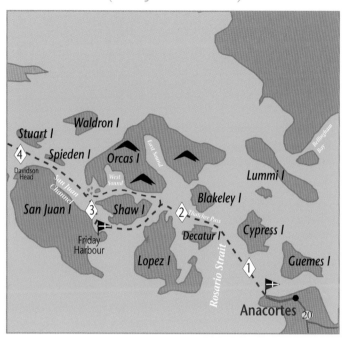

$\langle 2 \rangle$ Harbour seals and California and Steller sea lions *(in winter)* haulout onto the kelp-lined rocky shores of Thatcher's Pass. **S** Shoal Bay and Upright Head on Lopez Island are nesting sites for bald eagles. **N** Constitution, Turtleback and Orcas Knob Mountains ⌃ are on Orcas Island, the largest of the San Juans.

The ferry occasionally takes a route through Wasp Passage north of Shaw Island.

$\langle 3 \rangle$ **S** Friday Harbour is the site of the University of Washington Harbor Marine Laboratory and the Whale Museum. **W** Look for bald eagles, ospreys and great blue herons in San Juan Pass and on the Wasp Group of small islands west of Shaw Island.

$\langle 4 \rangle$ **N** Off Spieden Island, seals and sea lions haulout on rocks. **S** Note the sandstone formations of Davidson Head. In Haro Strait orcas congregate to feed on salmon migrating to spawn up the Fraser River. You might see Minke whales and Dall's porpoises.

$\langle 5 \rangle$ **S** The salt water lagoon protected by the sand spit on Sidney Island has concentrations of great blue herons.

from **Sidney**

29

Victoria to Seattle

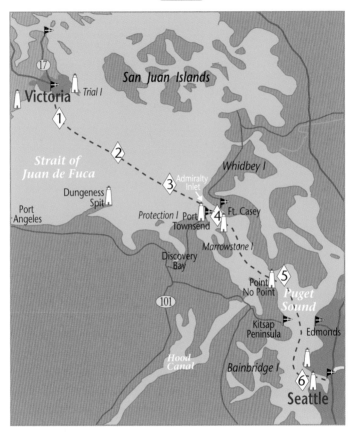

San Juan Islands

Trial I

Victoria

①

②

Strait of
Juan de Fuca

Dungeness
Spit

Port
Angeles

③ Admiralty
Inlet

Whidbey I

Protection I Port
Townsend

④ Ft. Casey

Marrowstone I

Discovery
Bay

Point
No Point ⑤

Puget
Sound

Kitsap
Peninsula

Edmonds

Hood
Canal

Bainbridge I

⑥

Seattle

Distance	145 km/90 miles
Crossing Time	2 hours *(passengers only)*
Operator	Victoria Clipper

Ft. Warden

This route traverses the exposed waters of Juan de Fuca Strait to enter the protected waters of Puget Sound. There is excellent marine mammal and bird viewing with views of Mt. Baker and Mt. Rainier. Victoria and Admiralty Inlet have historic military fortifications.

Bonaparte's gull

from **Victoria**

1 Victoria's glacier etched rocky shore has kelp beds, sea lions and seals, gulls, cormorants, bald eagles, harlequin ducks and scoters.
W of the harbour the gun batteries of Fort Rodd Hill and Fisgard Lighthouse ⌂ *(National Historic Site)* guard the naval base.
NE Over Trial Island ⌂ is Mount Baker, 130 km/80 miles distant.
S Above Port Angeles are the snow-capped Olympic Mountains.

2 N Look for the San Juan Islands and open ocean wildlife - seabirds *(shearwaters, petrels and murres)*, Dall's porpoises and occasionally an orca. Rarely you might see gray, humpback or Minke whales.

3 SW Protection Island *(National Wildlife Refuge)* is the nesting site for 75% of the seabirds in Puget Sound *(including tufted puffins)*. Discovery Bay was explored by Captains Quimper *(Spain, 1790)* and Vancouver *(England, 1792)*. **E** White silt bluffs fringe Whidbey Island. **S** Port Wilson ⌂ marks the entrance to Puget Sound.

4 W Port Townsend is separated by the tidal rips of Admiralty Inlet from **E** the gun batteries of Fort Casey Park (1898) and Keystone Harbour National Wildlife Refuge. **S** Marrowstone Point ⌂ has a dry rainshadow landscape – Douglas-fir and wildflower meadows. Look for boats fishing on Admiralty Bank for salmon and halibut.

5 S Mt. Rainier looms over Seattle. **W** is Point No Point ⌂ and the entrance to Hood Canal. **E** is Whidbey Island.

6 S The baseball stadium and the Space Needle are popular landmarks. **W** are Bainbridge Island and the Olympic Mountains. **E** West Point Lighthouse ⌂ and Magnolia Bluff *(misnamed for the madrone tree)* mark the approach to Seattle Harbour. Look for Dall's porpoises and gulls.

from **Seattle**

Vancouver - Nanaimo

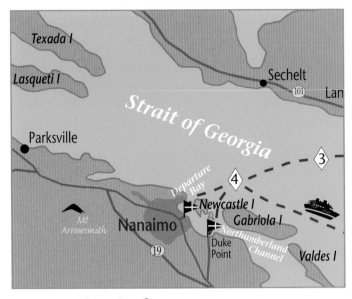

Distance	45 km/28 miles
Crossing Time	1 hour 35 minutes/1 hour
Operator	BC Ferries

Leaving the glacier-carved cliffs of Howe Sound *(a fiord)*, the ferry crosses the Strait of Georgia to reach the Gulf Islands protecting Nanaimo harbour. North and west are the dramatic backdrops of the snow-capped Coast Mountains and Vancouver Island Ranges. Northumberland Channel outside Nanaimo has concentrations of wintering sea lions and bald eagles.

from **Horseshoe Bay**

① **N** of ferry terminal, the waters of Howe Sound are subject to strong outflow winds. **NW** is Gambier Island. Ferry takes Queen Charlotte Channel between **W** Bowen Island and **E** West Vancouver. Watch for bald eagles, cormorants and gulls, and in fall murrelets, scoters, loons and other waterfowl.

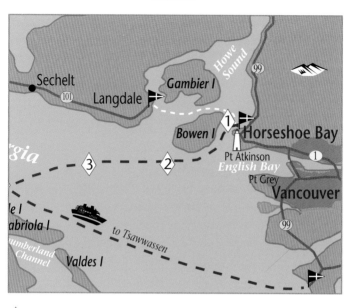

② **E** Downtown Vancouver, Lions Gate Bridge and Stanley Park. Anchored freighters in English Bay are framed by Point Atkinson to the north and Point Grey to the south.

③ **W** Distant Mt. Arrowsmith ▲ rises behind Nanaimo. Here you might sight orcas and dolphins. **N** are Texada and Lasqueti Islands.

④ **SW** The sandstone cliffs of Gabriola Island are summer nesting sites for bald eagles and peregrine falcons. **W** are Newcastle Island and the Departure Bay ferry terminal. In October, look and listen for seals, clusters of gulls and cormorants feeding on herring "balls".
S California and Steller sea lions congregate in winter in Northumberland Channel.

from **Nanaimo**

Whales

There are 20 species of whales found in the Salish Sea. In the right season and with proper arrangements you have an excellent chance of a sighting. A whale watching boat tour also offers the chance to see other marine mammals such as sea lions and seals.

Orcas

The orca or killer whale is actually a member of the dolphin family. This toothed whale is highly social and lives in permanent family groups or pods. The 300 resident orcas in the Salish Sea feed on fish, primarily salmon. Summer or early fall is the time to see orcas before they disappear for the winter. The best locations to see the southern resident population are the San Juan Islands and Victoria. Occasionally you might sight a

whale from shore or aboard a ferry. Orcas can also be seen from the town of Ucluelet as they travel up the west coast. The northern resident population is best viewed at Robson Bight Ecological Reserve on Vancouver Island, north of Campbell River. As land access is controlled, make arrangements with the local tour operators to see the orcas here.

Whales

There are also 150 transient orcas which pass through the Salish Sea or along the outer coast. These orcas feed exclusively on sea mammals including other whales. Sightings are unpredictable.

Gray whales

Each spring 20,000 gray whales migrate from Baja, California in Mexico along the coast to feeding grounds in the Bering Sea, returning south late in the year. Spring is the best time to view gray whales as they tend to move closer inshore. Gray's Harbour, Tofino and Ucluelet are good places to arrange a tour. Some whales enter the Strait of Juan de Fuca, where they can sometimes be glimpsed from shore off Sooke, Victoria or even Seattle. During summer a number of resident whales remain in bays along the coast to feed on rich bottom muds, thriving on clams, sea cucumbers and marine worms.

Whales

Humpbacked whales are occasionally seen in the Salish Sea. Another whale is the smaller **Minke whale** which commonly feeds in the tidal rips of northern Puget Sound and the San Juan Islands. These whales feed on zooplankton – shrimp-like copepods and amphipods, tiny crustaceans, small jellyfish and larvae of many species from crab to sea urchins to halibut. They feed by ingesting large volumes of water then squeezing it out through baleen which filters and traps the food.

Dall's porpoises at play

Porpoises and Dolphins

The dull-coloured **harbour porpoise** and the larger, white-marked **Dall's porpoise** can both be found around northern Puget Sound, the Gulf and San Juan Islands and Victoria. Like their much larger relative, the orca, they have a triangular dorsal fin. Look for them from the ferries. The playful **Pacific white-sided dolphin** is more likely to be seen in the northern Straits of Georgia.

Puget Sound Ferries

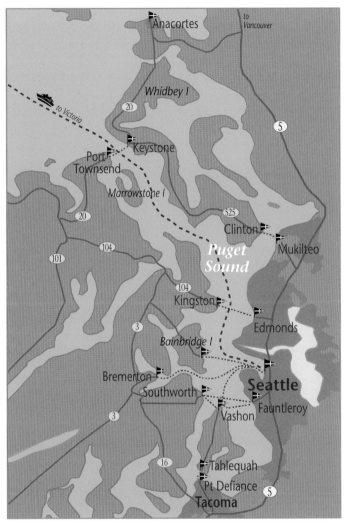

Operator Washington State Ferries

Southern **Gulf Island** Ferries

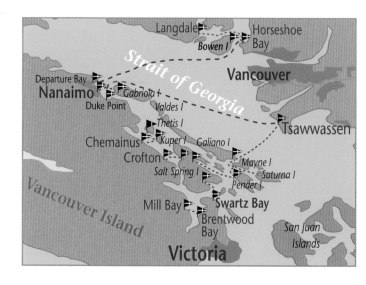

Operator   BC Ferries

Northern **Gulf Island** Ferries

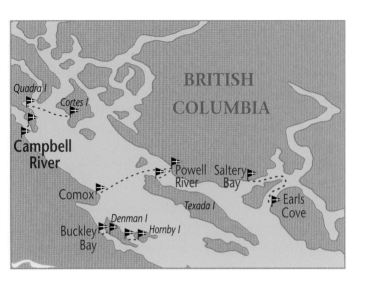

Quadra I
Cortes I
BRITISH COLUMBIA
Campbell River
Powell River
Saltery Bay
Comox
Texada I
Earls Cove
Denman I
Hornby I
Buckley Bay

BC Ferry - Gulf Islands

Operator BC Ferries

First Nations of the Salish Sea

The First Nations of the Salish Sea were saltwater peoples who made use of the varied marine and forest resources for food, as well as in their technologies and in their arts. Supported by an abundance of food, in particular salmon, a distinctive Northwest Coast culture developed with artistic expression in songs and dances, as well as in elaborate masks and other wood carvings. The social structure was based on the family and clan which owned specific fishing and harvesting sites. Wealth was distributed at the potlatch ceremony, at which the guests would receive numerous and valuable goods.

Food was obtained by fishing, hunting and gathering. Although farming was not practised, there was some management of the natural landscape. In the Garry oak meadows, burns were used to promote the growth of favoured edible plants such as blue camas and bracken fern. Herbs were collected for medicines from the forests.

fish weir Cowichan River

Language Groups

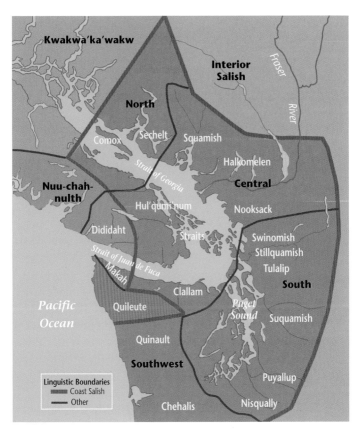

The Aboriginal peoples who owned the lands and seas around the Strait of Georgia and Puget Sound belonged to the Coast Salish language group, while the Nuu-chah-nulth ("Nootka") occupied Vancouver Island's outer coast and the Kwakwa'ka'wakw ("Kwakiutl") the north Island.

basket weaving

The Salish Natural Year

Wexes (March)
Frog moon. The first spring salmon are caught. Cedar boughs are put out to collect herring roe for drying. Ducks are netted for food and feathers.

Sxuel (April)
Bullhead or sculpin moon. These fish are found under intertidal rocks. Clams are dug from beaches during the low spring tides.

Pexsisn (May)
The sweet young green shoots from salmonberry, thimbleberry and cow-parsnip are picked, peeled and eaten. Deer and elk are hunted. Families move out to summer camps.

Penawen (June)
Harvest moon. Gull and duck eggs are gathered. Fishing begins for lingcod, rockfish, halibut and other bottom fish. Seals and porpoises are hunted. Sea lettuce and other seaweeds are collected. Common camas, chocolate and other lily bulbs are dug up, cooked and stored.

Centeki (July)
Sockeye salmon moon. Salmon are caught in river or reef fisheries and dried for winter use. Berry picking begins with salmonberries and strawberries. Cattails and tule (bulrush) are gathered to make mats. Cedar bark and cedar roots are collected.

Cenhenen (August)
Humpback (pink) salmon moon. Sealing and coastal whaling takes place. Blackberries and huckleberries are dried or made into jams.

Centawen (September)
Coho salmon moon. Gooseberry and salal berries, cranberries and Pacific crab apples and other fruits are collected. Roots such as arrowhead tubers, Pacific silverweed and lupines are dug and prepared for winter.

Pekelanew (October)
Leaves changing colour moon. Chum or dog salmon are gaffed in rivers. Families move back with supplies to the winter villages.

Wesa'new (November)
Shaker of leaves moon. Elk and deer are hunted. Ducks are netted. Foods are stored for winter.

Sjelcasen (December)
Time of winter dances moon. Storms restrict travel. Women's indoor work includes making baskets, mats and blankets. Stinging nettle is made into cordage.

Siset (January)
Long winter moon. Men's indoor work continues. Canoes, tools, and utensils are carved.

Ninene (February)
Young ones' moon. Signs of spring appear.

The Tree of Life

The western redcedar was central to the economic and social life of all the Northwest Coast First Nations. The wood of this large tree is light, easily split and highly decay resistant. It provided materials for many products. House planks were split from the living tree to construct longhouses measuring 10 m/33 ft by 20 m/66 ft. Large ocean going canoes, totem poles, masks and other carvings and

Cedar carving on wall of longhouse

bentwood boxes were also made from the wood. Bark was pulled off the living tree in long strips to weave mats, hats and rain capes. The roots were peeled to fabricate fine coiled baskets, while small branches were made into ropes and withes for constructing fish traps.

Forests and Trees of the Salish Sea

Even though your first impression might be of mountains and hills cloaked in a uniform evergreen forest, there are actually several types of forests in the region. Influenced primarily by differences in elevation and rainfall, each of these forests forms a distinctive habitat, recognizable through typical trees, shrubs and flowers. The table below is a simplified overview of the main forest habitats around the Salish Sea. Expect to see local variations, for example, along a creek or in a rocky upland where there are differences in drainage, soil quality and moisture.

mountain hemlock

Forest Habitat	Typical Trees
timberline 1,700+ metres 5,600+ feet	stunted subalpine fir
subalpine 1,000 - 1,700 metres 3,300 - 5,600 feet	mountain hemlock subalpine fir yellow-(Alaska) cedar
temperate rainforest 0 - 1,000 metres 0 - 3,300 feet	western hemlock Sitka spruce Douglas-fir western redcedar bigleaf maple red alder
rainshadow low elevations	madrone (arbutus) Garry (Oregon white) oak Douglas-fir

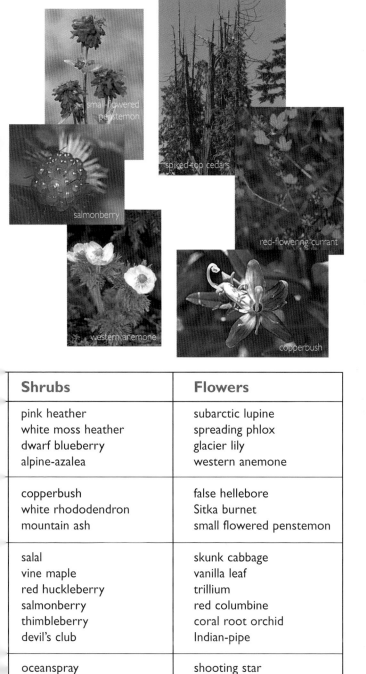

small-flowered penstemon

spiked-top cedars

salmonberry

red-flowering currant

western anemone

copperbush

Shrubs	Flowers
pink heather white moss heather dwarf blueberry alpine-azalea	subarctic lupine spreading phlox glacier lily western anemone
copperbush white rhododendron mountain ash	false hellebore Sitka burnet small flowered penstemon
salal vine maple red huckleberry salmonberry thimbleberry devil's club	skunk cabbage vanilla leaf trillium red columbine coral root orchid Indian-pipe
oceanspray hairy manzanita red-flowering currant Nootka rose	shooting star wild onion Puget Sound gumweed stone crop

Recognizing Trees

At first glance all the evergreen trees might appear as a type of "pine". Try sorting them out into their different species using the distinguishing features outlined below. Sizes can, of course, vary considerably. The heights in brackets are average for old growth trees, but on good growing sites where fire is absent, trees can grow much larger. Specimens of western redcedar, yellow-cedar, Douglas-fir and Sitka spruce over a thousand years old are among the largest living organisms on earth.

Evergreen Trees With Flat Sprays of Small Scale Like Leaves

Redcedar (60 m/200 ft) has soft leaves which are aromatic when crushed. Bark is gray and stringy and cones are small and egg-shaped.

Yellow-(Alaska) cedar (24 m/80 ft) has rough leaves. The outer bark is thin, gray-brown and brittle. The inside bark is yellow with a musty smell. Cones are small and round.

redcedar

western hemlock

Evergreen Trees With Single Needle-Like Leaves

Douglas-fir (85 m/235 ft) needles are flat and soft. The brown bark is thick and ridged. The 8 cm/3 inch cones have "squirrel tails". A grove of Douglas-fir has a pleasant sweetish smell.

Douglas-fir

Hemlock needles are different lengths, flat and glossy. The bark is reddish-brown, grooved and ridged. Cones are small and purple or green. The top of the tree droops. Includes **western hemlock** (50 m/165 ft) and **mountain hemlock** (30 m/100 ft).

shore pine

"True" firs have flat needles with notched tips. The smooth thin bark has resin blisters. The 8 cm/3 inch upright cones disintegrate on trees. Includes **grand fir** (80 m/265 ft), **amabilis fir** (50 m/165 ft) and **subalpine fir** (35 m/115 ft).

Sitka spruce (70 m/230 ft) has rough, four sided needles and is found in the coastal fog belt. The thin bark is scaly and gray-brown. The 5 cm/2 inch cones are reddish.

Pines with needles in bundles of 2 are **shore pines**, a small, crooked tree with very small cones. If needles are in bundles of 5 it is a **western white pine** (60 m/200 ft) which has very large cones.

Broad Leaved Trees

Bigleaf maple (35 m/115 ft) has large leaves (15-30 cm/6-12 inches), which turn yellow in autumn. The gray-brown bark is often covered with mosses, ferns, and lichens. It is a large spreading tree.

bigleaf maple

Red alder (24 m/80 ft) grows quickly and has bright green, oval leaves and thin, greenish/whitish bark. Fresh cut bark or wood bleeds bright red.

Garry (Oregon white) oak (20 m/66 ft) is the only oak leaved tree you will see locally. It has spreading, crooked branches and dark gray, grooved or scaly bark.

Madrone (arbutus) is the only local broadleaved evergreen. Notice the shiny oval leaves and thin, reddish peeling bark. White, fragrant flower clusters appear in spring followed by red berries in fall.

Route Index

Seasonal Highlights of the Salish Sea

Spring

- ✤ arrival of gray whales
- ✤ northward bird migrations:
  - Brant geese
  - rufous hummingbirds
- ✤ rainshadow wildflower blooming

Summer

- ✤ orca whale watching
- ✤ bears and deer
- ✤ songbirds
- ✤ nesting seabirds
- ✤ alpine wildflower blooming
- ✤ wild berries ripen
- ✤ best time for tidepooling
- ✤ kelp and other seaweeds at their peak
- ✤ shorebird southward migration commences

Fall

- 🍃 arrival of snow geese
- 🍃 gray whales start southern journey
- 🍃 spawning salmon arrive in rivers
- 🍃 southward bird migrations
- 🍃 mushrooms sprout with fall rains

Winter

- 🪶 arrival of California sea lions
- 🪶 winter storms on outer coasts
- 🪶 concentrations of overwintering birds:
  - bald eagles and hawks
  - snow geese, trumpeter swans and other waterfowl
- 🪶 spawning herring attract seals and birds

Practical Advice

Clothing West coast weather is moderate and variable. Sea level daily average temperatures range in July from a low of 10C/50F to a high of 20C/70F, and in January from 2C/36F to 6C/43F. Even in summer the ocean waters are cool, so on a boat or near the coast have a sweater or windbreaker handy. A good rain jacket and hat are recommended.

Footwear Wear a good pair of running or walking shoes. Hiking boots are suggested for more rugged trails, while rubber boots make tidepooling more comfortable.

Binoculars A good pair of binoculars will improve your opportunities to see wildlife.

Guide books There are many specialized field guides on birds, trees, plants and marine life available at bookstores throughout the region. These books are essential for detailed identification.

Camera or Video Recorder Be sure to have your camera or camcorder ready for photo opportunities.

Biting Insects Mosquitoes and blackflies can be a nuisance in some locations, such as mountains in summer. Bring insect repellent. There are no poisonous snakes.

Shellfish Poisoning Be cautious collecting shellfish for consumption. Check for posted notices or at fishery offices to see if the area is closed because of pollution or paralytic shellfish poisoning *(caused by red tide, a naturally occurring algae)*. Be sure to get a licence and check the opening for each area.

Walks and Hikes Stay on marked trails and make sure you return during daylight. The CasualNaturalist's Guide IS NOT INTENDED FOR WILDERNESS HIKING. If this activity interests you, buy a specialized guidebook and a good local topographical map, and enquire locally about weather and trail hazards.

Respect Ownership For the most part, the sites described in this guide are in parks or on public lands. You need permission to access or cross privately owned lands or First Nation Reservation Lands.

Conservation Limit your impact. Park rules generally prohibit any type of collecting as well as encourage you to stay on marked trails in fragile environments. These are also good habits in any environment.

Use common sense when visiting any of the sites described in the Guide. Stay on marked walking trails and allow sufficient time to return to your starting point during daylight. Although a number of the recommended stops also serve as trailheads to wilderness areas, this Guide is not intended or suitable for wilderness hiking. If you are interested in these rougher trails or in multi-day trekking, enquire locally about conditions, and be sure you are prepared and capable. Even close to cities such as Vancouver and Victoria, the terrain can be rugged and it is easy to become lost.

On coastal walks pay careful attention to the tides and weather. Exercise caution if you venture beyond a headland at low tide, as you might be cut-off at high tide. Strong currents and beach logs make it inadvisable to swim or wade on the beaches exposed to heavy surf. These beaches are found on the outer Pacific coasts of the Olympic Peninsula or Vancouver Island.

As the primary purpose of this book is that of a natural history guide, it is meant to be supplemented by a current highway map. Current information on ferry route schedules, parks and other attractions or facilities can be obtained from the operators or agencies listed in the back of this book.

Introduction to the Road Routes

There are many different routes and byways worth exploring for their scenic values and for the opportunity to see wildlife. Using the excellent network of highways and by roads, you can follow coastlines, explore the many islands, visit pristine lakes or ascend into the high mountains. Road routes which share similar natural history features are found together in the same sections in the Guide. Introducing each section is a brief description of the characteristic habitats found along the routes.

Using the Maps and Descriptions

Each road route is introduced with an overview which provides general directions and features of interest. Accompanying most routes is a directional map *(which should be supplemented by a current British Columbia and Washington State highway map)*. Each route has descriptions of recommended sites where you can stop to see wildlife, wildflowers or other natural history features. Wildlife symbols indicate what you can expect to see. Sites with interpretive centres, indicated by a symbol, are staffed and have local maps and guides available for free or purchase.

Pacific Flyway Route

Between Seattle and Vancouver are some of the most remarkable birding sites found on the North American continent. Large numbers of birds migrate through, overwinter or breed in the Salish Sea. It is an important stop for several million waterfowl and shorebirds migrating on the Pacific Flyway from the Arctic to California, Mexico and Central and South America. Fall

black turnstones

migrations begin with the shorebirds in July. September and October bring migrating ducks, then geese and swans until numbers and species peak in November. The spring migration to the northern breeding grounds lasts from mid-March to mid-May. It tends to be less conspicuous. Snow geese and trumpeter swans are some of the many species which arrive to overwinter. Other fall and winter viewing opportunities include hawks and owls. Summer is a quieter season when migrant and overwintering birds depart from the estuaries.

Shorebirds and waterfowl are best viewed at high tide when they are closer to the shore. Take the opportunity to visit the freshwater lakes and marshes in the region as these too are

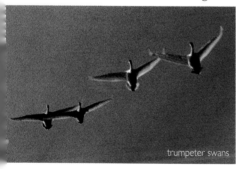
trumpeter swans

important stops for migrating birds.

Estuary Habitat

The rich estuaries and deltas of the Salish Sea make it one of the six most important regions for birds in the Americas. High rainfall and deep mountain snowpacks load rivers and streams

great blue heron in flight

with sediments which are deposited in river mouths. Orcas, sea lions, snow geese, sandpipers, bald eagles, and salmon depend on a food chain supported by the microscopic bacterial and planktonic life found in healthy and productive estuaries. The survival of the remaining undeveloped wetlands is crucial to the future of survival of the unique ecology of the Salish Sea.

San Juan river estuary

Tidal Flats

The tidal flats found in estuaries are among the most productive plant communities on earth. If you visit a tidal flat, notice the separate zones or habitats.

tidal marsh

Closest to you and highest above the waterline is the tidal marsh consisting of plants tolerant of the brackish water. The seeds, shoots and roots of cattails, sedges and bulrushes provide food for ducks, geese and swans. The edible sea asparagus, which is found growing in beds with other plants in shallow lagoons, is also an important food source for wildlife.

Visible only at low tide is the next habitat, the unvegetated mud flats. Siphon holes indicate the presence of numerous clams, while sand castings are evidence of many species of polychaete worms living in the mud. Large concentrations of edible blue mussels, snails, soft shelled clams, ghost shrimp, lugworms and proboscis worms provide food for millions of migrating shorebirds.

The third habitat is formed by the subtidal beds of eelgrass, a flowering plant which has evolved to grow under water. Look for the leaves of this true grass floating on the water's surface or washed up on a beach after a storm. Worthy of close investigation, eelgrass beds teem with life, providing food and shelter for many animals. Migrating Brant geese feed almost exclusively on eelgrass. Crabs, including the large edible Dungeness, frequent the beds. In the mud are ghost shrimps and, above all, countless numbers and species of worms. Perch, pipe fish, smelt and juvenile salmon shelter and feed here.

Seattle to Vancouver

Skagit Wildlife Area

Leave Hwy 5 at Conway *(Exit 221, 8 km/5 miles south of Mt. Vernon)* and follow Fir Island Road to reach the Skagit Delta. Look for red-tailed and rough-legged hawks, bald eagles and harriers in the flats. Tundra and trumpeter swans and snow geese overwinter here, with large numbers of ducks and other waterfowl.

Padilla Bay National Estuarine Research Reserve

American avocet

North of Mt. Vernon, exit Hwy 5 at either Hwy 20 or at Burlington. Go west to Bayview State Park and the Breazeville Interpretive Centre. Extensive tidal flats and eelgrass attract waterfowl such as the Brant goose, canvasbacks and harlequin ducks, bald eagles and peregrine falcons.

Boundary Bay Wildlife Management Area

North of the US/Canada border, follow Hwy 99 and exit at Hwy 10 *(Ladner Trunk Road)*. Go north *(parallel to Hwy 99)* and take one of the farm roads west to the Boundary Bay dike. If you are coming south from Vancouver on Hwy 99, take the exit to the Tsawwassen Ferry. Then take the Hwy 10 turnoff and go south *(Ladner Trunk Road)*. The Management Area has the highest number of overwintering birds recorded in Canada, as well as extensive salt marshes, mudflats and eelgrass beds. It is noted for shorebirds such as western sandpipers and raptors such as the snowy owl.

Reifel Migratory Bird Sanctuary

Take Hwy 10 *(Ladner Trunk Road)* west through the town of Ladner and follow 47th Avenue and River Road West until you reach Westham Island Road. Turn right over the bridge and follow the signs. Over 230 species of birds have been recorded migrating or nesting here. In

Canada geese

October and November snow geese feed here before moving south to the Skagit Delta.

bald eagle

wood duck

wild lupines

trumpeter swans

Indian paintbrush

turkey vulture

pink mountain heather

false hellebore

gray jay

Douglas aster

owl clover

58

Sea to Mountain Routes

Where else can you begin your morning watching seals, gulls and great blue herons and then arrive a few hours later in the mountains above the treeline? The routes described in this section

black-tailed deer

have two of the most outstanding habitats in the region for seeing wildlife as they follow the rivers from the estuaries, where they meet the ocean, to their sources high in the mountains above. Estuaries are interesting sites year-round for birds and small mammals, but are exceptional for birding during fall and spring migrations. In the mountains you can see large mammals such as black bears and black-tailed deer, and upland birds such as blue grouse and ravens. Alpine wildflower meadows are best visited in mid-summer, but late summer and early fall present the subtle colours of changing foliage and ripening berries. Look for the changing scenery and forest types in the transition zones between estuary and alpine habitats.

Comox estuary & Comox glacier

Mountain Habitats

The mountains surrounding the Salish Sea are among the snowiest places on earth. While you might think of glaciers in the context of cold, arctic climates, it is the huge snowfalls which develop the numerous glaciers found in the Olympic, Cascade and Coast Mountains, and the Vancouver Island Ranges. This combination of mild climate with high snow and rainfall creates unique coastal mountain habitats, quite distinctive from other mountains such as the Rockies to the east.

The subalpine forest forms at elevations above 1,000 m/3,300 ft where annual snowfalls often exceed 10 m/33 ft. The only trees which survive here are those which do not break under heavy loads of wet snow (mountain hemlock, yellow-cedar and subalpine fir). In the forest openings are wet fens or marshy areas with specialized plants including sedges such as narrow-leaved cotton grass, Sitka burnet and false hellebore. On drier sites, Sitka mountain ash and huckleberries are sought out by bears fattening up in late summer. Shrubs such as white rhododendron and copperbush can make hiking almost impassable. As you stop to picnic, the whiskey jack will boldly steal food out of your hand.

timberline heathland

As you climb above 1,700 m/5,600 ft, the subalpine forest becomes patchy and gives way to the timberline habitat. In this parkland, stunted trees grow in "islands", spring comes late and the spectacular flower blooms of summer are compressed into a few short weeks. Surprisingly the limiting factor for tree growth is not cold temperatures, as in most mountain habitats, but a short growing season due to deep snow. Here minor

common raven

changes in terrain have a major impact on the plant community. For example, south or west facing avalanche chutes or rock slopes are warmed early by the sun. Meadows of grass are found here, and flowers such as western anemone and glacier lilies bloom even before the snow has all melted. Shrubs such as pink heather and blueberries grow in profusion. Among the orange and red lichen-covered rocks are spreading phlox and other alpine flowers. Marmots, warning the rest of the colony of hawks overhead, give themselves away by their whistles.

Glacial and Island Ecology

During the last glacial period, only a few mountain tops on the Olympic Peninsula and Vancouver Island remained ice-free. At these sites a few animals and plants survived to evolve as unique species found nowhere else in the world. Examples are the Olympic marmot, the Vancouver Island marmot *(one of the rarest mammals in the world)*, and the Olympic harebell. Both these areas also show the effects of "island ecology" due to their physical isolation from the mainland. After the

spreading phlox

depopulation of animals and plants caused by glaciation, certain species such as grizzly bears, mountain goats, pikas and porcupines never reestablished themselves west of Puget Sound and the Strait of Georgia.

Nisqually National Wildlife Refuge to Mt. Rainier National Park

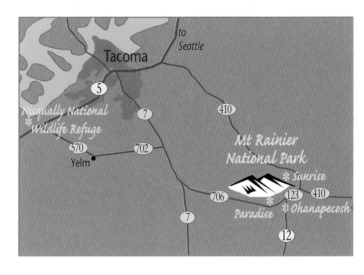

From Nisqually National Wildlife Refuge, located off busy Hwy 5 between Tacoma and Olympia, it is a pleasant, if circuitous drive, to Mt. Rainier National Park. Take Hwy 507 to Yelm and McKenna and go east on Hwy 702 in order to reach Hwy 7. Then continue on to the Nisqually Entrance to the park

Mt. Rainier

(open year-round). Along the way, take time to notice the madrone and Garry oak meadows found here. They are more typical of the Puget Trough rainshadow habitat to the south and the Gulf and San Juan Islands to the north. There is also a more direct route to the park which follows Hwy 7 south from Tacoma for 110 km/70 miles. In summer, you can return to Tacoma by exiting the park at the White River Entrance and following Hwy 410. Mt. Rainier is a 2 hour drive from Seattle.

Nisqually National Wildlife Refuge

bald eagles

The delta of the Nisqually River, which has its source on Mt. Rainier, is excellent year-round for observing bald eagles, great blue herons and songbirds. In spring and fall, there are large concentrations of ducks. With its visitors' centre and network of trails and observation spots, this site is a refreshing oasis in the built-up region of south Puget Sound.

Mt. Rainier National Park

whiskey jack

Mt. Rainier is highest of the active volcanoes that stretch north from Mt. Hood in northern California to Mt. Garibaldi in British Columbia. Views of the 75 glaciers encircling the peak are only one reason it is heavily visited in summer. The 95,000 ha/ 235,000 acre park has 4 visitor centres and 300 miles of trails. Paradise and Sunrise Visitor Centres give you convenient access to alpine meadows where wildflower displays peak in July. You can see mountain goats, black-tailed deer, elk, marmots and Douglas squirrels. The route through the park from the Nisqually Entrance to the White River Entrance traces the transition from old growth rainforest habitat *(at Ohanapecosh Visitor Centre)* to subalpine habitat *(at Paradise Visitor Centre)*, reflecting the change from the wet west to the drier alpine zone at Sunrise on the east side of the Mountain. The sheer size of Mt. Rainier creates its own weather – 28 m/ 93 ft of snow fell at Paradise in 1971/72.

hoary marmot

Dungeness National Wildlife Refuge to Hurricane Ridge
(Olympic National Park)

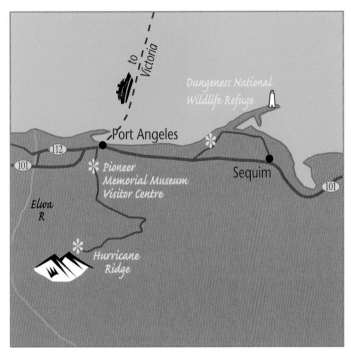

Dungeness National Wildlife Refuge and Hurricane Ridge Visitor Centre are separated by 45 minutes, 56 km/35 miles and a 1,580 m/5,230 ft change in elevation. Each site is worth a day visit on its own. Dungeness NWR is located on Kitchen-Dick Road 5 km/3 miles from the town of Sequim off Hwy 101. The

Hurricane Ridge Parkway is 27 km/17 miles west of Sequim in the direction of Port Angeles.

Dungeness National Wildlife Refuge

In the rainshadow of the Olympic Mountains is the flat prairie to the west of Sequim. It ends in high, soft bluffs of glacial deposits which overlook the Strait of Juan de Fuca. Wave erosion and prevailing currents moved the sands and gravels to create Dungeness Spit, one of the longest in the world. The enclosed bay and tidal flats are the estuary of the Dungeness River. Here, eelgrass beds provide a nursery for salmon and steelhead and food for Brant geese. Concentrations of other waterfowl such as harlequin ducks overwinter here. Present all year are loons, murrelets, cormorants, scoters, various gull species, great blue herons and other birds along with seals and sea lions. Sharp-shinned hawks and grouse might be seen in the adjoining Recreation Area.

Brant goose

Hurricane Ridge

glacier lily

The 30 km/18 mile drive up the Hurricane Ridge Parkway has remarkable views of Dungeness Spit, Victoria, the San Juan Islands and Mt. Baker. Notice how the forest habitats change with increasing elevation from a lowland zone of hemlock and redcedar, through the Douglas-fir zone and ending with mountain hemlock, yellow-cedar and subalpine fir at the visitor centre. Here the summer drought - winter rain climate gives rise to extensive meadows, quite different from the other alpine areas of the Salish Sea. During June or July, among glacier clad peaks and alpine bowls, you will be rewarded by a spectacular profusion of wildflowers in bloom. A network of paths leads to tree islands and alpine tundra. You can see black-tail deer, Roosevelt elk, black bears and small mammals such

Hurricane Ridge

as Olympic chipmunks. Listen for the whistle of the Olympic marmot. Turkey vultures, Coopers hawks, whiskey jack or gray jay, blue grouse and horned larks are some of the many bird species which populate this environment.

river otter

pine siskin

western sandpiper

spring gold

Canada goose

Lichens

There are thousands of types of lichens found in the diverse habitats and clean air of the Salish Sea. Conspicuous on bare rocks in the tide zone, on coastal bluffs and in the alpine regions, lichens are also common on trees and fallen logs in open woods.

lichens on rock

black tar

lipstick cladonia

coastal reindeer

leaf lichen

Squamish to Whistler

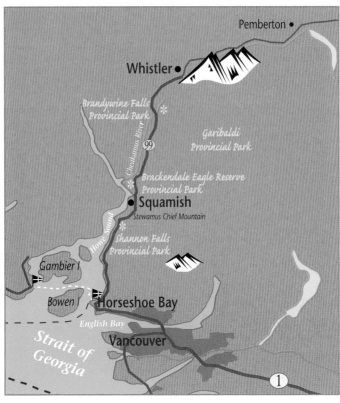

Pemberton •

Whistler •

Brandywine Falls
Provincial Park

Garibaldi
Provincial Park

Cheakamus River

99

Brackendale Eagle Reserve
Provincial Park

• Squamish
Stewamus Chief Mountain

Howe Sound

Shannon Falls
Provincial Park

Gambier I

Bowen I Horseshoe Bay

English Bay

Vancouver

Strait of
Georgia

1

Hwy 99 from Vancouver to Whistler has 120 km/75 miles of incredible scenery including many good examples of the geologic forces shaping the Salish Sea. From Horseshoe Bay to Squamish the road hugs the sheer cliffs of Howe Sound, a

glacier carved fiord. Stopping at **Shannon Falls Provincial Park** you can witness the erosive power of heavy rainfalls as rivers tumble to the sea. Rising above Squamish is the massive granite **Stawamus Chief**. North of the town is Mt. Garibaldi, a dormant volcano.

Pacific dogwood

In 1855, 25 million cubic metres of lava rock from Mt. Garibaldi crashed down Rubble Creek to where the hydro dam now sits beside Hwy 99. This columnar basalt rock is found along the road and in the canyon at **Brandywine Falls Provincial Park.** It crystallized into honeycomb formations as molten lava from the volcano flowed through mile deep glacial ice.

bald eagle

Squamish

Brackendale Eagle Reserve Provincial Park is the world's top wintering site for bald eagles – 3,701 were counted one day in 1994. Coinciding with the December and January salmon runs, eagles can be seen in abundance from Hwy 99 or side roads leading to the Squamish River.

Whistler

You will find many places to hike in Whistler, from semi-urban to wilderness trails. Black bears and black-tailed deer are common.

pika

Cougars are elusive. At an elevation of 350 m/1,150 ft the valley floor still remains under maritime influences, and remnant stands of old growth redcedar can be seen at Cougar Mountain and on Rainbow Lake Trails. In summer you can conveniently and effortlessly reach mile-high mountain meadows and glaciers via the Blackcomb or Whistler Mountain ski lifts. From the lift look down to see the transition of the forest from yellow-cedar and mountain hemlock, to subalpine tree islands and finally, above the timberline, to a profusion of heathers and other flowers characteristic of alpine tundra. Here, with luck, you might hear the whistle of a pika among the rocks.

Sitka mountain ash

Courtenay/Comox to
Mt. Washington/Paradise Meadows
(Strathcona Provincial Park)

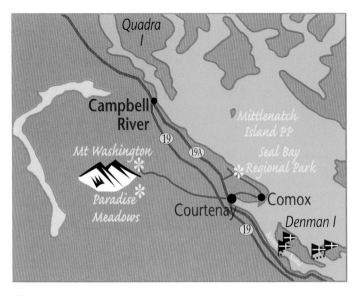

The Comox River estuary is located between the adjoining towns of Courtenay and Comox. While you are here, visit the **Puntledge River Fish Hatchery,** the nearby fossil digs (arranged through the **Palaeontology Museum** in Courtenay) and **Seal Bay Regional Park** north of Comox.

Comox Estuary and Area

Comox glacier

The estuary's modest appearance belies its interest and importance. Concentrations of wintering trumpeter swans, the largest waterfowl in the world, rest and preen in the estuary and feed in farm fields off the road to the ski hill. Other species found here include bald eagles, loons, grebes, scoters and sanderlings.

From Courtenay, follow the signs for 25 km/16 miles to the Mt. Washington ski hill. In summer, the ski resort runs the chair lift to the summit where there are unrivalled views of the Vancouver Island Ranges, Comox Glacier, the Gulf Islands and the mainland Coast Mountains. Here you can walk among the stunted trees, heathers and blueberry bushes typical of a treeline habitat. Look for whiskey jacks, ravens, Steller's jays, and goshawks.

The ski resort borders Forbidden Plateau, part of 210,000 ha/519,000 acre **Strathcona Provincial Park**. Here at 1,100 m/3,600 ft you can visit a subalpine forest, mountain meadows and lakes. Paradise Meadows has a network of self-guiding trails and board walks. It is a comfortable way to see how the huge coastal winter snowfalls affect vegetation. In the wet meadows and fens, among the yellow-cedar, subalpine fir and mountain hemlock, are sedges, Indian hellebore and partridgefoot. Abundant huckleberries and other foods support black bears, white-tailed ptarmigan, band-tailed pigeons and chickadees. Wolves and cougars are more secretive than the bears and black-tailed deer found in the park.

common harebell

Douglas squirrel

Juan de Fuca Routes

Starting from Victoria or Port Angeles you can follow the coasts of the Strait of Juan de Fuca to the open waters of the

chiton & starfish

Pacific Ocean – and you can return in a single day. Both these routes traverse a variety of habitats and offer interesting wildlife viewing opportunities. Travelling west, the vegetation changes from rainshadow to rainforest where black-tailed deer or bears might be seen. Deeply indented bays alternate with headlands where an orca or gray whale might be glimpsed.

There are superb tidepools, and excellent opportunities to see seabirds and raptors both along the way and at Botanical Beach and Cape Flattery. These sites, exposed to the full force of the open ocean at the mouth of the Strait, have breathtaking scenery.

turkey vulture

Juan de Fuca shoreline

red huckleberry

black-tailed buck

Puget Sound gumweed

beach pea

salal flowers

Rocky Shore Habitat

Rocky shorelines are found on the headlands of the outer coast and the Strait of Juan de Fuca, in the Gulf and San Juan Islands, and on the east shore of the Strait of Georgia north of

black oystercatchers

Vancouver. While each shoreline has its own special characteristics, all share the distinctive features of the rocky shore habitat.

Here, in the narrow band between forests and the tide zone, flowers and shrubs have adapted to survive in small pockets of soil exposed to wind and salt spray. Shore pines, salal and Nootka rose grow gnarled and twisted. Seaside plantain, sea blush, coastal strawberry and stonecrop flower among the rocks. Look for yellow monkey-flower, deer fern and blue green algae beside fresh water seeps. Black-tailed deer and Douglas squirrels are common.

Nootka rose

river otters

You will see many species of birds. Black oystercatchers feed on shellfish and nest on bare rock. Pelagic cormorants, marbled murrelets and tufted puffins frequent the waters. Barred owls hunt silently in the forests. River otters and sea lions patrol the edges of kelp beds bordering the shore.

Rocky Shore Habitat

decorator crab

The greatest variety of intertidal life is found on rocky shores. In wave and current swept sites every square inch of rock in the low tide zone is covered in luxuriant layers of seaweeds. Many of these algae, including sugar kelp and nori, are edible. Even the undersides of rocks form a distinct habitat populated by sponges, chitons and clingfish.

stonecrop

clingfish

Intertidal Life

As the tides rise and fall twice daily, you might notice that the exposed intertidal life varies by location. This is due to differences among sites in the underlying physical structure, in the amount of exposure or protection from waves and currents, and in the salinity of the water. Three of these different habitats are easily recognized.

Open beaches on the outer coast are very scenic, but are challenging environments for plants and animals. Waves constantly shift the sands and grind gravel and cobbles together making it difficult for organisms to gain a stable foothold or to avoid being crushed and ground in winter storms.

Protected mud and sand flats found in bays and estuaries may look bleak, but actually are very rich and productive habitats. They are challenging to examine close-up, and are a fragile and easily disturbed habitat.

Rocky shores provide diverse micro-habitats to shelter numerous plants and animals. When you compare sites on the rocky shores of the San Juan and Gulf Islands to sites on the shores of the Strait of Juan de Fuca and the outer coasts, you will observe differences in the tidal life. Sites on the shores of the islands have greater protection from waves and currents, and the water in the Gulf of Georgia and Puget Sound is less salty.

Tips on Tidepooling

Whether or not you had a previous interest in marine biology, you will no doubt be fascinated tidepooling at one of the many superb sites in the Salish Sea or on the outer Pacific Ocean coast. But don't ignore the importance of timing, safety and conservation.

Check the tides

There are two high and two low tides each day. Consult the tide tables for your site to determine the time of the low tide. Ideally your visit should be timed so that the low tide is under .9 m/3 ft in Canada, or under 2.1 m/6.8 ft in the US *(tides in each country are recorded differently)*. Local tide tables can be found at fishing stores or in local newspapers. The best seasons to tidepool are spring and summer when low tides occur during daylight hours. It is best to time your visit to start with an outgoing tide.

Safety

Remember that tides come back in! Check your location constantly to make sure you will not be cut-off from your return route by the high tide. Know how to recognize locations subject to heavy surf. Never turn your back to the ocean on the exposed outer coasts, as dangerous rogue waves can appear without warning.

Conservation

A few simple rules will avoid damage to plants and animals, and help conserve a tidepool site for others:

- avoid walking on animals
- don't collect live specimens
- return specimens to their natural habitats
- fill in holes dug in the beach
- turn upturned rocks back over and replace the seaweed cover

Recognizing surf and surge prone sites

Gooseneck barnacles, California mussels, red sea urchins, surf grass and sea palm are warnings that a site is exposed to dangerous waves or surges.

Identifying the Intertidal Zones

Beaches and rocky shores are separated into distinct zones according to the length of time each zone is covered by water or exposed to air.

spray zone *(lichens, periwinkles)*

layers of lichen

Descending bands of gray, orange and black lichens mark and subdivide the spray zone. Only the ocean spray or the highest storm waves reach this zone. Plants and animals found here must survive extremes of heat and cold, salt spray, rain and long, dry periods.

high tide zone *(limpets, sea tar lichen, brown rockweed, common acorn barnacles)*

rockweed

Uncovered at low tide, plants and animals in this zone depend on high tides to provide nutrients and food. The acorn barnacle survives above the range of its predator, the purple sea star.

middle tide zone *(purple sea star, blue mussels, aggregating anemones, coralline algae, feather duster worms, and mossy chiton)*

purple sea star

Here a great variety of plants and animals are covered and uncovered daily. The chiton, a mollusk with overlapping plates, feeds on algae. The purple sea star, which feeds on shellfish, is only one of many sea stars in the Salish Sea.

low tide zone *(red sea urchin, giant green sea anemone, brittle sea star, Dungeness crab, sand dollar, orange sea cucumber, red sponge, surf grass)*

giant green anemone

Covered except during the lowest tides, this crowded intertidal zone has animals and plants normally seen only by scuba divers.

periwinkles

plate limpets

acorn barnacles

sea star lichen

aggregating anemone

coralline algae

mossy chiton

feather duster worms

blue mussels

red sponge

surfgrass

brittle sea star

sea cucumber

sand dollars

mottled sea star

79

Victoria to Port Renfrew

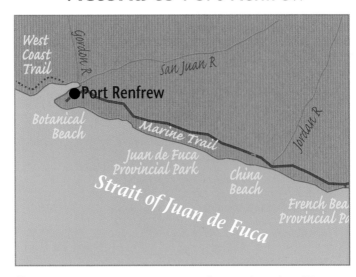

From Victoria, it is 110 km/70 miles (about 2 hours) on Hwy 14 to Port Renfrew. Along the way are a number of sites worth a stop. You can see fall salmon runs at **Sooke River Potholes Provincial Park**. **Whiffen Spit**, protecting Sooke Basin, attracts birds in all seasons. Port Renfrew is at the estuary of the Gordon and San Juan Rivers. This is the south end of the famous **West Coast Trail** *(Pacific Rim National Park)*. This rugged trail is a 75 km/47 mile wilderness hike to Bamfield (permits needed, reservations recommended). You can enquire locally about short day hikes in the Port Renfrew area, such as to the Red Creek Douglas-fir. This tree, with a circumference of 1,250 cm/492 inches, is still 73 m/240 ft tall even with a broken top.

East Sooke Regional Park

Turn off Hwy 14 at Kangaroo Road and follow the signs to either the Aylard (east) or Pike Road (west) entrance to this large semi-wilderness park. There are trails through forest, marsh and field, and

common raven

along the rugged coast. Here you will find spring and summer wild flowers, seals, sea lions, otter and black-tailed deer. You might see a gray whale in spring or an orca in summer. This is the only location in the Salish Sea where each fall hundreds of hawks and turkey vultures "kettle", waiting for the right wind current, at land's end before migrating south across the Juan de Fuca Strait.

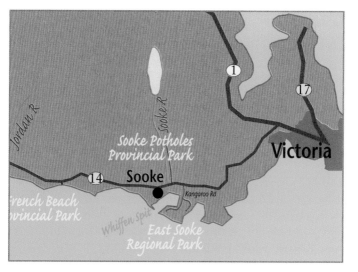

French Beach Provincial Park

The park provides easy access to a cobble beach. There are fossilized shells in the sandstone formation at the west end, and Sitka spruce and salal in the salt spray zone behind the beach. In spring you might spot an occasional gray whale.

China Beach and Juan de Fuca Marine Trail Provincial Park

This area has hemlock forests, rocky headlands, beaches and tidepools. China Beach is a 15 minute walk from the parking lot. **Mystic Beach**, a rougher 45 minute hike from a separate parking lot, is the start of the 47 km/29 mile long **Juan de Fuca Marine Trail**, a 3 day wilderness hike ending at **Botanical Beach**.

osprey

Botanical Beach (Juan de Fuca Provincial Park)

Beautiful sandstone and shale rock formations, open to the ocean, form basins like miniature aquariums which are exceptional for tidepooling. Check tide tables to time an excursion with the low tide. You can take a short, and not too difficult hike, along the forested shoreline.

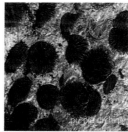

purple urchins

Port Angeles to Neah Bay

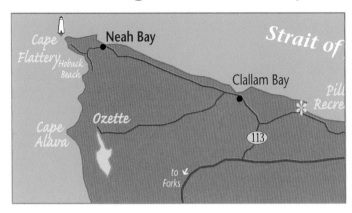

Hwy 12 west of Port Angeles has wonderful views of the Strait and Vancouver Island. It is 120 km/75 miles (a 1.5 hour drive) to Neah Bay on the Makah Indian Reservation. Along the way stop at **Clallam Bay** to see the fossil beds visible at low tide past the Slip Point lighthouse. Consider taking the Ozette Road turnoff for the 15 km/9 mile round-trip hike to the beaches at **Ozette-Cape Alava** *(Olympic National Park)*.

Salt Creek Recreation Area

The protected sandy bay at Crescent Beach adjoins the surf-swept rocks and tidepools of Tongue Point. Here you can see bull kelp and other seaweeds, anemones, and auklets, murres, oystercatchers and other shore and seabirds.

Pillar Point Recreation Area

Dungeness crab

Sheltered between two headlands, with mud and sand tidal flats to the west, and mud flats and rocks to the east, this large bay is very enjoyable for bare foot tidepooling among seaweeds, eelgrass and clam beds. Many varieties of invertebrates such as crabs and sea stars are visible here, along with great blue herons and bald eagles.

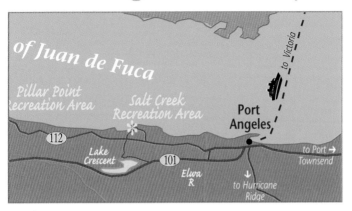

Cape Flattery - Hobuck Beach
(Makah Indian Reservation)

In the village of Neah Bay is the **Makah Museum** with its unrivalled collection of well-preserved artifacts excavated from a 300 year old buried village. Whale watching tours can be arranged from here. South 10 km/6 miles, is Hobuck Beach and the **Makah National Fish Hatchery**.

Here you can explore tidepools, and see sea otters, shorebirds and migrating waterfowl. Gray whales swim inshore. Turn north just before Hobuck

Cape Flattery

Beach, to reach Cape Flattery, the northwest tip of the lower 48

tufted puffin

states. The lookout, perched on a spectacular cliff, is a pleasant 20 minute walk through the forest from the parking lot. There are stunning views of **Tatoosh Island**, sea stacks and sea caves. You will see large numbers of tufted puffins and cormorants.

Rainshadow Routes

In the shelter of the Olympic Mountains, the Vancouver Island Ranges and the Coast Mountains, exceptional wildflowers are to be seen in spring and early summer. There are grass meadows and Douglas-fir forests. Shorelines are protected and vary from beaches to silt bluffs to lichen-banded rocky shores. Here you can conveniently combine a coastal drive with a short ferry ride to create an excellent opportunity to view a variety of wildlife. The Whidbey Island and Saltspring Island Routes can be done as day excursions from Seattle or Victoria. Plan the other routes as part of a longer itinerary.

Victoria shoreline

harvest brodiaea

California quail

Rainshadow Habitat

hummingbird nest

The Gulf and the San Juan Islands, southeast Vancouver Island, and the northeast Olympic Peninsula all receive less than 75 cm/30 inches of rain per year. This winter wet and summer dry habitat has the widest variety of plants found in the Salish Sea.

Garry oak and madrone trees are found at low elevations on well-drained sites. In spring and early summer, meadows are covered in blooms - chocolate lily, wild onions, harvest brodiaea, white fawn lily, satin flower, shooting star and blue-eyed-Mary. The Salish people used burns to maintain the open meadows where they harvested the roots of the common camas and hunted deer. Moss and lichen covered rock-balds are green in winter. In spring, these sites are draped in wild flowers, attracting

Garry oak meadow

swallowtails, Lorquin's admiral and other butterflies. In summer, the grasses yellow and die, and prickly pear cactus and stonecrops bloom on rocky outcrops.

Open evergreen forests of Douglas-fir and madrone can be seen from the ferries passing through the Gulf and the San Juan Islands. Rufous hummingbirds arrive each spring to feed on the early blooming redflowering currant. Pacific rhododendron *(Washington's State Flower)*, oceanspray, wild blackberry, western trumpet honeysuckle, mock orange, Oregon grape and Pacific dogwood

ocean spray

(BC's Provincial Flower) are other typical shrubs. In low-lying damp locations the Douglas-fir is found with redcedar and sword fern.

This ecosystem has the greatest number of endangered plants in the region. It is threatened by urban development, logging, fire suppression and introduced species of plants and animals.

Garry oak acorn

sea blush

common camas

Oregon gumweed

red paintbrush

madrone

madrone on mossy bald

spreading stonecrop

nodding onion

Oregon grape

shooting star

edible thistle

hairy manzanita

Whidbey Island

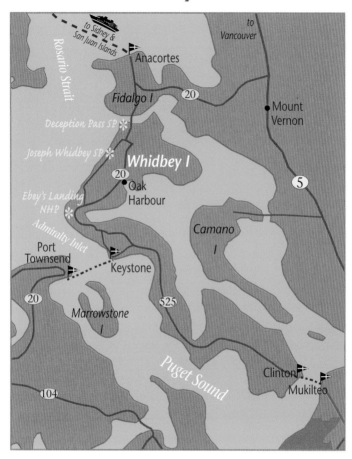

The idyllic scenery and ambience of Whidbey Island attract many visitors in summer. Here you can see rhododendrons in

Douglas-fir forests. Whidbey Island is also a convenient hub to reach other destinations. Hwy 20 takes you to Anacortes *(the ferry terminal for the San Juan Islands and Vancouver Island)* and Keystone, *(the ferry to Port Townsend)*. Further south the Clinton Ferry returns you to Hwy 5.

wild lupine & buttercup

Deception Pass State Park

Separating Fidalgo and Whidbey Islands, Deception Pass has diverse intertidal life due to strong tidal currents. The park features freshwater lakes, Douglas-fir forests, madrone trees and spring wildflowers.

purple seastar

Joseph Whidbey State Park

Migrating birds feed at the wetlands of the park. **Smith Island National Wildlife Refuge**, only 5 km/7 miles offshore, is an important nesting site for rhinoceros auklets, tufted puffins and black oystercatchers.

Ebey's Landing National Historic Park

Here you can experience a small vestige of the original prairie grasslands which were found in the Olympic rainshadow.

Keystone & Keystone-Port Townsend Ferry

Begin this 35 minute ferry ride at Keystone Harbour. Look east to view the driftwood beaches of Admiralty Bay and the marshes surrounding Crocket Lake where kingfishers, great blue herons and bald eagles congregate. Frequently you can see Dall's porpoises, a great variety of marine birds and even orcas on the ferry ride across turbulent Admiralty Inlet.

great blue heron

Clinton-Mukilteo Ferry

On the ferry across Possession Sound you might see Minke whales, Dall's porpoises or California sea lions. The eelgrass beds and rich marine life found here result from the mixing of the Snohomish River with salt water.

Saltspring Island

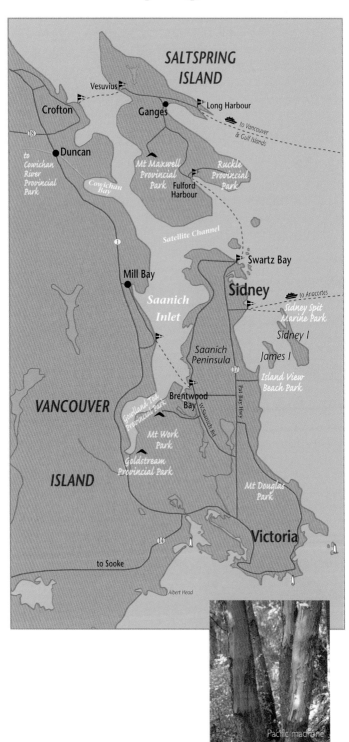

Pacific madrone

Saltspring, largest of the Gulf Islands, is named after the pools at its north end. The name also suggests the summer water shortages common in the rainshadow habitats. You can reach Saltspring from Victoria either by going north on Hwy 1 past Duncan to the ferry terminal at Crofton, or by taking the Pat Bay Highway to the ferry terminal at Swartz Bay.

moon snail & mantle

Crofton-Vesuvius Bay Ferry

During the 20 minute passage across Stuart Channel you might see seals, porpoises and bald eagles as well as seabirds. From Vesuvius drive east past Mary Lake to either Long Harbour *(ferry terminal for Vancouver and other Gulf Islands)* or the town of Ganges and its pleasant harbour walkway.

Mt. Maxwell Provincial Park

Take Cranberry Road to reach this park. Its hiking trails take you through moss and grass meadows among the Douglas-fir and madrone trees. At the peak are spectacular views of Saltspring and other islands. There is excellent wildflower viewing in spring and early summer.

rainshadow forest

Ruckle Provincial Park

West of Fulford Harbour is the largest park in the Gulf Islands. A Douglas-fir forest and open meadows of madrone and Garry oak overlook a rocky shore, where you can find intertidal life typical of the sandstone coastlines found on the Gulf Islands.

pileated woodpecker

Fulford Harbour-Swartz Bay Ferry

Take this 35 minute passage to see seals, Dall's or harbour porpoises, cormorants, loons, gulls, terns and bald eagles.

Exotic Species

The Salish Sea's wealth of natural resources and its temperate climate and beauty have attracted rapid population and economic growth. Landscapes have been modified by large scale forestry, urban development and industrialization. Some introduced plant and animal species are now so widespread that you might mistake them for native species.

Scotch broom and **gorse** were introduced for landscaping because of their fast growth and bright yellow flowers. These noxious, if attractive weeds, choke out native rainshadow habitats and forest regrowth.

gorse

Japanese oysters and **Manilla clams**, staples of the shellfish industry, are commonly found on beaches on the inner coast. Culinary appreciation aside, they are not native species.

European starlings form large flocks as they prepare to roost at the end of a winter day and usurp nesting sites favoured by native birds.

The **eastern gray squirrel** is common in urban parks. Favoured by human development it out competes the less aggressive, native Douglas squirrel and Steller's jay for hazelnuts and other food.

The **mountain goat** is native to Mt. Rainier and the Cascade and Coast Mountains. Yet it has caused serious damage to fragile mountain habitats since its introduction to Olympic National Park.

Victoria to Swartz Bay

There are a number of sites worth visiting on the Saanich Peninsula off the Pat Bay Highway *(Hwy 17)* which goes from Victoria to the BC Ferries terminal at Swartz Bay.

To reach the famous **Butchart Gardens** exit the Pat Bay Highway at Keating Cross Road and follow the signs. Also off Pat Bay at McKenzie Avenue is **Swan Lake** and **Christmas Hill Nature Sanctuary**.

Sidney Spit Marine Provincial Park

Turn off Pat Bay Highway and drive through Sidney to the end of Beacon Avenue. In summer a water taxi takes you to the park on Sidney Island. You can see murres, scoters and loons on the water. Sand beaches and tidal flats offer wildflower and salt marsh plant viewing. The lagoon is a feeding site for great blue herons.

Gowlland Tod Provincial Park, McKenzie Bight and Mt. Work Regional Parks

These three parks on the Saanich Inlet encompass the north end of the "sea to sea greenbelt", a vast park network surrounding Victoria. From Butchart Gardens follow West Saanich Road south to Willis Point Road; or from Victoria, take Hwy 17 north to the Royal Oak exit to West Saanich Road. Follow Willis Point Road to the entrance to these parks. Mt. Work Park is a demanding climb through a Douglas-fir forest to rocky outcrops of moss, madrone, manzanita and typical local summer wildflowers. Alternatively, take the other direction from the parking lot, and follow the trail down to McKenzie Bight on

madrone

Saanich Inlet to see a wet lowland forest of redcedars and bigleaf maples. You may also see river otters, mink and seals in the little bay. Only the physically fit will want to climb the rough trails of Gowlland Tod Park which borders Saanich Inlet.

Victoria to Nanaimo

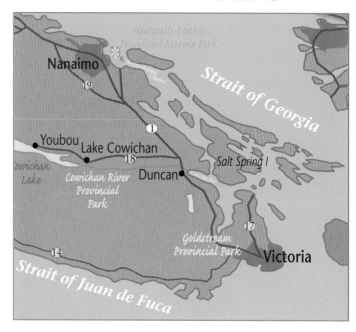

Goldstream Provincial Park

Turn off Hwy 1 at Finlayson Arm Road, 19 km/12 miles north of Victoria to reach this compact park with both lowland and rainshadow forest. It has elevation changes from sea level to 416 m/1,359 ft. From October to December, chum salmon spawn in Goldstream River accompanied by gulls, bald eagles and an occasional black bear. A short walk through old growth forest with ancient cedars will take you to the interpretative centre and estuary.

white trillium

deer fern

satin flower

Cowichan River Provincial Park (Duncan)

North of Duncan take Hwy 18 west to Lake Cowichan and follow the signs to the Cowichan River Park where a footpath follows this salmon river. In Duncan see the **Freshwater Eco-centre and Hatchery**. Visit the estuary at nearby Cowichan Bay.

A word of caution, if you are considering travelling west on Hwy 18 to the ancient rainforest valley at Carmanah Provincial Park, the saltwater Nitinat Lake, or the coastal area of Bamfield. The roads beyond Lake Cowichan are poorly marked, unpaved, rough and shared with large logging trucks.

Cowichan River

chanterelle mushrooms

Nanaimo - Newcastle Island Provincial Marine Park and Northumberland Channel

In summer take the 10 minute water taxi from **Maffeo Sutton Park** *(just before the BC Ferry Departure Bay terminal in Nanaimo Harbour)* to car-free Newcastle Island. Bald eagles, peregrine falcons, pelagic cormorants and pigeon guillemots nest in the rocks and cliffs lining Northumberland Channel. Seals and tidepools are other attractions. Note the sandstone geology of the Nanaimo Lowlands of eastern Vancouver Island and the Gulf Islands. Coal and fossil outcrops are common.

From late October to March over 2,000 California and Steller sea lions congregate with bald eagles and waterfowl in Northumberland Channel. They are attracted by the herring spawn which occurs in January and February. Take the **Gabriola Island Ferry** from the harbour or visit the Nanaimo River Estuary at Harmac near the BC Ferries Duke Point terminal to see the sea lions.

osprey

Nanaimo to Campbell River

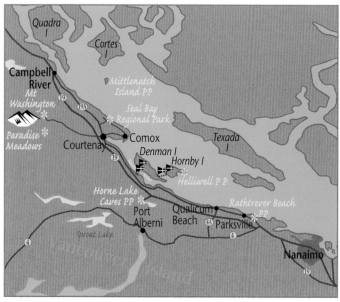

Every February through March a natural history phenomenon takes place between Nanaimo and Campbell River as Pacific

glaucous-winged gull

herring spawn in the bays and harbours. The herring attract tens of thousands of gulls, loons, scoters, oldsquaw ducks, along with other diving ducks, Steller and California sea lions, and harbour seals. Another spectacle occurring from October to February in the small rivers flowing into the Strait of Georgia, are the salmon runs. The area has excellent beachcombing in summer.

Be sure to detour off the Island Highway (Hwy 19) by taking the Parksville or Fanny Bay exit in order to drive along the shore on old Hwy 19A.

barn swallow

Rathtrevor Beach Provincial Park

The Parksville/Qualicum Beach area is a stopover from March to May for 20,000 Brant geese migrating from Mexico to the Arctic. Over 240 species of birds occur in this area.

Brant geese

Horne Lake Caves Provincial Park

Large limestone caves are found in the Quatsino Formations of northern Vancouver Island. North of Qualicum Beach follow the signs west to Horne Lake. The area has trails and undeveloped caves open to the public. Coho salmon can be seen in the Qualicum River in late fall.

Baynes Sound

Exit Hwy 19 at Fanny Bay to visit Baynes Sound. Shallow and rich in clams, mussels and crabs, this site attracts thousands of diving birds which can be viewed from the road or the ferry to **Denman Island**. Another short ferry ride brings you to **Hornby Island** and **Helliwell Provincial Park**.

Courtenay/Comox to Campbell River

Comox Harbour is a superb site for viewing waterfowl and seals. Enquire locally about the hiking trails found throughout the Comox Valley. This region has many examples of freshwater, coastal forest, subalpine and timberline habitats.

Mittlenatch Island Provincial Park

cormorants

This large seabird colony has nesting pelagic cormorants, black oystercatchers, glaucous-winged gulls and pigeon guillemots. Boat tours are available from Campbell River.

Vancouver to Comox

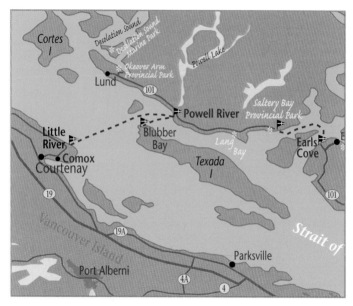

The 150 km/95 mile long Sunshine Coast, sheltered by Vancouver Island and the Coast Mountains, has a mild climate, spectacular fiords and rocky headlands. The gravel shores, muddy bays and sandy beaches support a large number of clams and oysters. To reach Sechelt, 2 hours north of Vancouver, take the ferry from Horseshoe Bay. Powell River, a further 4 hours by road and ferry, is also linked by ferry to Comox on Vancouver Island.

Horseshoe Bay-Langdale Ferry

The massive mountain to the north is Tetrahedron Peak. On the 20 minute ferry across Howe Sound look for gulls and cormorants, and in winter, scoters, loons and grebes.

swallowtail

Smugglers Cove Provincial Park

This small scenic park is 14 km/9 miles north of Sechelt. Take a 20 minute hike through forests to the headlands and the cove. Along the rocky shores you will see flocks of surfbirds and black turnstones in spring, murrelets in late fall, and ducks and bald eagles in winter.

via **Sunshine Coast**

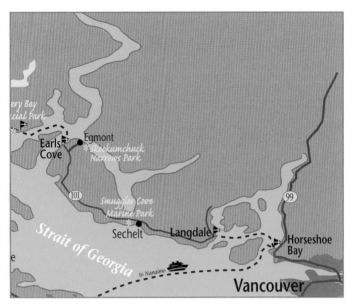

Skookumchuck Narrows Provincial Park

Here the waters fill and drain Sechelt Inlet twice daily. From Egmont, take a 45 minute walk to view the 10-14 knot tidal current and 5 m/15 ft standing waves. The narrows are rich in intertidal life.

Earls Cove-Saltery Bay Ferry

The 50 minute crossing of Jervis Inlet offers possible sightings of orcas and sea lions. Earls Cove and **Saltery Bay Provincial Park** are good tidepooling sites. **Lang Creek** salmon spawning channel attracts bald eagles.

Powell River-Comox Ferry

You might spot an orca on the 75 minute ferry ride to Vancouver Island. The ferry passes north of the old whaling station at Blubber Bay on Texada Island. There is superb mountain scenery to the west and east. Hwy 101 ends 28 km/18 miles north of Powell River at Lund. **Okeover Arm Provincial Park**, popular with kayakers accessing **Desolation Sound Provincial Marine Park,** has unrivalled scenery. In summer, the waters are surprisingly warm.

killdeer

coastal canopy

banana slug

Indian-pipe

villous cinquefoil

salal berries

Rainforest and Open Coast **Routes**

The west coasts of the Olympic Peninsula and Vancouver Island are unrivalled for wild scenery. On the Olympic Peninsula, the beaches in the north are framed by headlands and sea stacks,

Rialto beach

while further south they tend to be longer and more open. The Vancouver Island coast is broken up into many fiords, islands, and protected sounds which are ideal for boat tours. In the west-facing valleys on both the Olympic Peninsula and Vancouver Island you can visit surviving examples of ancient rainforests.

An ideal summer day often begins cloaked in sea fog, which burns off by noon revealing a clear blue sky. But be prepared for wet weather. These coasts are open to the North Pacific Ocean. In winter, storm watching is an attraction. Travel on these routes should be planned around one or more overnight stays.

Roosevelt elk

Temperate Rainforest Habitat

The world's most impressive temperate rainforests are found in close proximity to the Pacific Ocean on narrow coastal plains

beard lichens

and in valleys below elevations of 330 m/1,100 ft. Here trees attain massive sizes due to mild winters, annual rainfall of 3 m/10 ft and infrequent forest fires. The delicate flowers found in these fog-bound forests seem overwhelmed by the greenery of trees, mosses and ferns.

Western hemlock, the most widely distributed tree, is found with Douglas-fir in drier locations and with western redcedar and amabilis fir in more humid settings. Another characteristic rainforest tree, Sitka spruce, grows on well-drained valley flood plains. It is also found on gravel or sand terraces back of exposed coastal beaches where it grows with salal, another plant tolerant of salt spray. Never far inland is the shade-loving western yew. Tree seedlings and red huckleberry take root on fallen "nurse logs". After the nurse log has rotted away, the young trees are arranged in colonnades or rows, often with trunks suspended by buttressed roots.

nurse log

Hanging from branches in more open forests are lichens such as Methuselah's beard and witch's hair. Along river edges the trunks of bigleaf maples are covered with licorice fern and moss. In wetter areas you will find red alder, skunk cabbage, calypso orchid and shrubs such as devil's club, gooseberry and salmonberry.

old growth

calypso orchid

skunk cabbage

barred owl

With trees older than a thousand years, unlogged old growth forests are irreplaceable. This special habitat is essential for the survival of native birds such as the western screech-owl, the marbled murrelet and the pileated woodpecker. Shade tolerant western hemlock and sword fern grow below the forest canopy providing food for Roosevelt elk and black-tailed deer. Cougars, black bears, squirrels and martens share these forests. The lungless western red-backed salamanders, and other small creatures, are underfoot feeding on a myriad of invertebrates, many of which are yet to be discovered by scientists.

A common animal in this perpetually humid environment is the banana slug. It grows to 25 cm/12 inches making it the largest land mollusk in the world. Mushrooms and other fungi grow in the rotting vegetation of the shaded forest floor. Look for odd flowers lacking green leaves and chlorophyll such as Indian-pipe and coral root orchid. These saprophytes obtain their nutrients from the rotting vegetation.

banana slug

coral root orchid

Open Beach Habitat

The sand and cobble beaches of the outer coasts are challenging habitats for plants and animals. Look in the protected pockets found among the bleached logs driven high up the beach by

strong winds and surf. You will find searocket, beach pea and other plants. In the sand above the high tide line are dunegrass and the large-headed sedge. You will notice this grass-like plant if you step on the sharp fruiting spikes with bare feet. In spite of heavy rains, these plants have had to develop long tough root systems to find water. The roots also serve to stabilize the sand dunes against waves and wind.

sand verbena

Nuttall's cockle

On a sandy beach, the tide zone appears barren. But notice the feeding sanderlings, gulls and crows who move in advancing and receding lines following the waves. Razor clams, tube worms, ghost shrimp and beach hoppers are among the diverse small burrowing animals in the intertidal zone. Surf perch and sole are some of the fish, while moon snails and sunflower stars are examples of invertebrates which feed here – arriving and departing with the tide. In summer, you can often find moon and come-by-wind jellyfish blown ashore.

moon snail & sand dollar

California gull

The smooth bleached rocks on a cobble beach may also appear barren. But the beds of gravel and sand protected underneath the larger rocks can be surprisingly rich in life. Purple shore crabs, butter clams, horse clams, peanut worms and many other burrowers thrive here.

cockle & clam shells

purple shore crab

sand dollars

Olympic Coastline

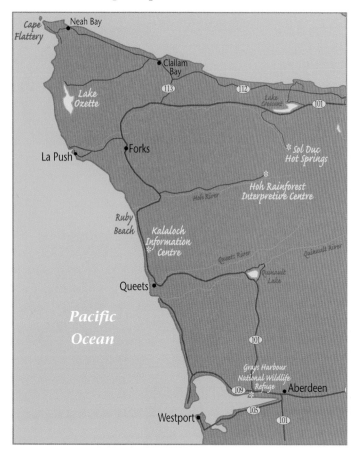

Olympic National Park, established in 1938, was declared a World Heritage Site by UNESCO in 1981. The nearly one

Hurricane Ridge

million acres, most protected as pristine wilderness, encompasses a remarkable range of habitats - mountain, rainforest and coastal zones. You can comfortably visit timberline and subalpine habitats at Hurricane Ridge. Most alpine and glacier habitats can only be reached through hundreds of miles of trails leading into the interior of the park. There are 90 km/57 miles of coastline in the park. The offshore is protected as the Olympic Coast National Marine Sanctuary.

and **Hoh** Rainforest

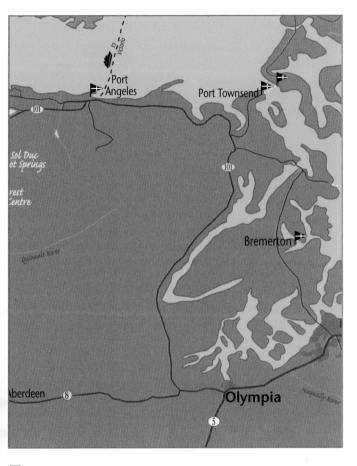

The highlight of this route will be your visit to the temperate rainforest and the Olympic coast. From Port Angeles to Aberdeen, the route follows Hwy 101 in and out of the National Park boundaries, with side trips to Sol Duc, La Push and Hoh. With so many beautiful sites to visit, plan to take at least two days to travel this 230 km/145 mile route, but be advised that accommodations outside of Port Angeles and Aberdeen are limited.

La Push sea stack

Lake Crescent, 40 km/25 miles west of Port Angeles, is the largest lake in Olympic National Park. There are walking trails

Sol Duc falls

here, including one to the 27 m/ 90 ft **Marymere Falls**. Enquire at the Storm King Information Centre about educational activities. Past the lake you will come to the turnoff to the Sol Duc Hot Springs. The 20 km/12 mile road to the hot springs meanders through rich forest lowlands of old growth Douglas-fir. Stop halfway at **Salmon Cascades** on the Sol Duc River. Just past the resort the road ends at the head of a 1.5 km/1 mile trail to **Sol Duc Falls**, a pleasant walk under massive Douglas-fir and hemlock trees.

Continuing west on Hwy 101, near the junction of Hwy 113 is the **Sol Duc Salmon Hatchery**. You might also consider taking a side trip west to **Neah Bay** or **Lake Ozette**.

La Push

La Push

To reach La Push, continue on Hwy 101 for 45 km/28 miles west of the turnoff to Sol Duc. Just before you reach Forks, turn off Hwy 110 and take the south arm of the road where it splits with Quillayute Road. Then there is a second branch. Take the north arm *(Mora Road)* to **Rialto Beach**. Or you can take the south arm of the road *(La Push Road)* to visit the small fishing village of La Push on the Quillayute Indian Reservation and **Second Beach** or **Third Beach**.

This scenic area combines sea stacks, a small estuary, tidepools, headlands and open beaches. Protecting the village are the steep walls of James Island, part of the reservation land. You can see California sea lions, seals, river otters, sea otters and in spring even gray whales offshore. Ospreys, bald eagles, gulls, cormorants and other birds are common. The offshore islands are protected as part of the **Olympic Coast National Marine Sanctuary**. In the tidepools are urchins, anemones, sea stars, and many shellfish and algae. Kelp beds are plentiful.

anemone & starfish

The cobble shore of Rialto Beach separates the ocean from the Quillayute River. Notice how the salt spray tolerant Sitka spruce grows back of the beach. If you wish to tidepool, go north on the beach to **Hole in the Wall**. Second Beach is sandy, but if you continue south, a short walk leads to spectacular **Teahwit Head** with its many tidepools. Further south is Third Beach. Notice the convoluted layering of the rock exposed by waves on the heads and sea stacks. This layering was caused as sediment, deposited by rivers in the ocean, hardened and was scraped to the surface by the subduction of the Juan de Fuca Plate, under the North American Plate.

Hoh Rain Forest

In the west-facing valleys of the Hoh, Queets, and Quinault Rivers stand still-magnificent remnants of the temperate rainforest valleys which once stretched from Oregon to Alaska. Here trees grow to massive sizes because of the mild temperatures and an annual precipitation over 350 cm/140 inches. The Hoh Valley is the most accessible of the three.

Hoh Rain Forest Interpretive Centre is a 30 km/18 mile drive off Hwy 101. The turnoff is 24 km/15 miles south of Forks or 21 km/13 miles north of Ruby Beach. Hall of Mosses and other interpretative trails meander among the dominant spruce and western hemlocks with Douglas-fir, redcedar and bigleaf maples. A record-sized western hemlock, with a circumference of 686 cm/270 inches, towers 73 m/241 ft. Here you can visit the biggest Douglas-fir in the park. This tree is 90 m/298 ft tall with a circumference of 1,183 cm/448

inches. Ferns, mosses, lichens and vanilla leaf carpet the forest floor. Roosevelt elk and river otters frequent the river edge where you can see harlequin ducks and spawning salmon. Look for black-tailed deer, Douglas squirrels, kinglets and banana slugs. Present, but elusive, are black bears, cougars and the spotted owl.

vanilla leaf & bracken fern

Ruby Beach to Kalaloch

Hwy 101 parallels the Hoh River from Forks to Ruby Beach. From Ruby Beach to the **Kalaloch Information Centre,** the road follows a bluff above sandy beaches piled high with bleached logs. There are several stops with beach access. You might

glimpse a gray whale offshore during the spring migration.

Quinault Lake

To reach Lake Quinault, turn off Hwy 101 51 km/32 miles south of Kalaloch *(77 km/48 miles north of Aberdeen)*. A 45 km/27 mile loop of the lake on the north and south spur roads leads to the less visited **Quinault Rain Forest**. Nearby you can see a record sized Sitka spruce standing 58 m/191 ft with an impressive circumference of 1,796 cm/707 inches.

Grays Harbour

From Olympia, take Hwy 8 west to Grays Harbour. To reach the north shore from Aberdeen/Hoquiam take Hwy 109 west. Here you can visit **Grays Harbour National Wildlife Refuge**, a large estuary with exceptional birding, and Ocean Shores Peninsula, well known for migrating sandpipers in fall and winter. To reach the south shore from Aberdeen/Hoquiam, take Hwy 105. At **Westport** arrangements can be made in March, April and May for gray whale watching boat tours, or look for California sea lions, seals and marine birds from the town jetties.

pileated woodpecker

rosehips

giant green anemone

anemone

purple violet

blood star

wild strawberry

blue mussels

red columbine

Pacific Rim National Park

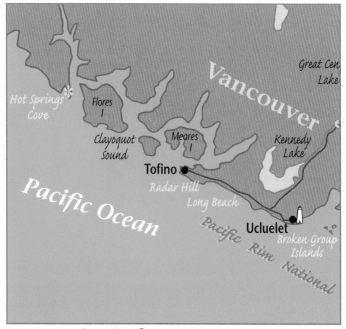

Pacific Rim National Park includes islands, headlands, coves and beaches representative of the Pacific coastline of Vancouver Island. The park is divided into three distinct units: **Long Beach, Broken Islands Group** and **Cape Beale and the West Coast Trail**.

Long Beach is the easiest section of the park to access and has services nearby in the towns of Tofino or Ucluelet. There are many year-round activities, from tidepooling and bird watching, to forest

walks and fall or winter storm watching. You can explore the scenery and wildlife found offshore and on the islands by arranging a boat tour from either Tofino or Ucluelet. This is also the best means to see migrating and resident gray whales from spring through fall. Cape Beale and the north end of the West Coast Trail are located just outside **Bamfield** on the south shore of **Barkley Sound**.

northern flicker

As access to Bamfield is on rough gravel roads, it is recommended that transportation be arranged from Port Alberni or Victoria. Alternatively take the MV Lady Rose or the MV Frances Barkley from Ucluelet or Port Alberni.

Pacific Rim National Park

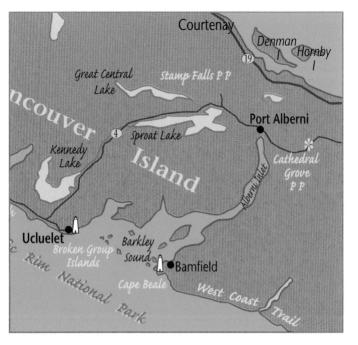

The 130 km/80 mile scenic drive to **Pacific Rim National Park** meanders past beautiful lakes, rivers and snow-capped mountains as well as through logged and regenerating forests. Exit the Island Highway *(Hwy 19)* and follow Hwy 4 west. Note how the Douglas-fir growth on the drier eastern slopes of Vancouver Island changes to western hemlock and western redcedar on the wetter western slopes. A popular stop is **Cathedral Grove Provincial Park** - a vestige of old growth forests. **Port Alberni** is located at the head of Alberni Inlet, longest of the many fiords on the Island's west coast.

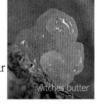

witches butter

The Stamp and Somass Rivers have sockeye, coho and chinook salmon runs from July through December which attract seals and bald eagles. Best viewing is at **Stamp Falls Provincial Park** 11 km/7 miles north of

Sproat Lake

Hwy 4. When you reach the junction of Hwy 4 and the Tofino-Ucluelet Hwy, turn north to go to Long Beach, Tofino and **Clayoquot Sound**. Turn south to reach Ucluelet and **Barkley Sound**.

Long Beach and Wickaninnish Visitor Information Centre ◈

The Wickaninnish Centre, located at the south end of Long Beach, provides information on services, the Pacific Rim National Park's natural history and on local First Nations. Here you can walk onto the south end of 20 km/12 mile Long

Schooner Cove

Beach, which has wide white sands framed by rocky headlands. There are numerous sites to explore in this section of the park. **Schooner Cove** and **Box Island** are excellent for tidepooling. **Radar Hill** overlooks coastal bogs with spiked-top redcedar trees and gives a 180 degree view of the ocean and coast.

Tofino and Clayoquot Sound

gooseneck barnacles

Tofino, just outside the north end of the park, is the gateway to the islands and coves of Clayoquot Sound, including **Hot Springs Cove**. Extensive tidal flats between Tofino and Meares Island offer productive birding. You might also see the occasional orca whale.

Ucluelet and Barkley Sound

Amphritrite Point, just south of Ucluelet, marks the entrance to Barkley Sound. Visit the viewpoint at the lighthouse. This is the best site for viewing migrating gray whales and the occasional orca whale pod.

keyhole limpet

Boating the Outer Coast

A boat will significantly add to your appreciation of the diverse scenery, habitats and wildlife of Clayoquot and Barkley Sounds. Arrangements can conveniently be made in Tofino or Ucluelet

a variety of seaweeds

for whale watching or other guided tours on boats that range from enclosed water taxis to rigid hulled inflatables. It is also possible to rent a motorboat or a kayak. While parts of the Sounds are sheltered by many islands, others are open to the full force of the Pacific Ocean. A relaxed alternative is to take the **Lady Rose** or the **Frances Barkley**. These small freighters run down Imperial Channel from Port Alberni to Bamfield and Ucluelet.

In Barkley Sound you can visit the **Broken Group of Islands**. This site is frequented by Steller sea lions, seals, sea otters and a

variety of marine birds, including ocean species such as fulmars and shearwaters *(in summer)*. Seaweeds grow as profuse

carpets of colour sheltering other rich intertidal life. You might also find abandoned Native village sites, whaling stations and canneries.

North of **Campbell River**

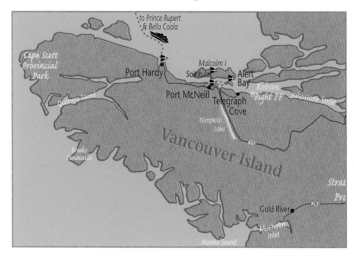

Campbell River marks the north end of Georgia Strait and the beginning of Johnstone Strait. For the visitor prepared to travel a little bit off the beaten path, the town serves as a gateway to many remarkable locales. A word to the wise, north and west of Campbell River distances are long, and services are less frequent. Local weather, often damp in summer, turns wild and fierce in winter. **Cape Scott** at the tip of Vancouver Island is 533 km/ 333 miles north of Victoria.

Campbell River-Quadra Island-Cortes Island Ferries

Take the BC Ferries from Campbell River across Discovery Passage to Quadra Island to observe strong currents, whirlpools and standing waves created as tides flow in and out of the Strait of Georgia. This is an important route for salmon migrating south to spawn in the Fraser River and other smaller waterways which empty into Georgia Strait and Puget Sound. Look for orcas, sea lions and seals. From Quadra Island, another short ferry ride takes you across Strait Channel to **Whaletown** on Cortes Island. Here, isolated from tidal surges, waters become quite warm in sheltered bays, sandy lagoons and rocky coves. Cortes Island has 3 Provincial Parks - **Mansons Landing, Smelt Bay,** and **Von Donop Marine Park.**

North of **Campbell River**

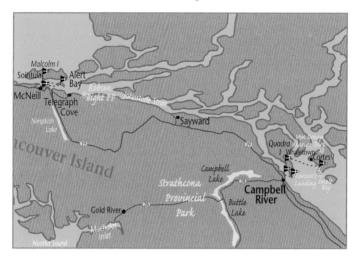

Strathcona Provincial Park (Buttle Lake) and Gold River (Nootka Sound)

If you go west from Campbell River for 45 km/30 miles on Hwy 28, you will arrive at Buttle Lake in Strathcona Provincial Park *(B.C.'s oldest provincial park)*. South along the lake are nature walks, as well as trailheads for wilderness hiking in the alpine environment. West on Hwy 28 is **Gold River** at **Muchalat Inlet** on the Pacific Coast, where passengers can travel up the coast to Nootka Sound on the boat, **MV Uchuck**.

Robson Bight Provincial Park

North of Campbell River is the best site in North America to see orca whales as they come to rub on the gravel beaches at Robson Bight Provincial Park. Controlled access requires taking a tour boat from **Sayward** *(79 km/50 miles north of Campbell River)*, **Port McNeill** or **Telegraph Cove** *(197 km/125 miles)*.

Port Hardy - BC Ferry - Prince Rupert & Bella Coola

Port Hardy, 230 km/144 miles north of Campbell River, marks the end of Hwy 19. It is the terminal for the BC Ferries northern routes. The **Inside Passage** is a 15 hour voyage to Prince Rupert through the sheltered waters and fiords of BC's northern coast. BC Ferries **Discovery Coast Passage** travels to the mid-coast, stopping at a isolated Native villages before reaching Bella Coola. Depending on the ports of call, the voyage lasts from 12 to 21 hours.

Life Cycle of Salmon

The annual salmon migrations symbolize the biological richness of the Salish Sea. Born in fresh water, these fish migrate to the sea to mature. Each year five different species of salmon reenter local streams and rivers in order to spawn at the exact location where they hatched from eggs. They spawn in the

spawned chum salmon

nests or redds which the female excavates in shallow gravel beds, then they die. Nutrients from the decaying salmon carcasses support plankton which feed the hatching fry until they grow into larger smolts. Depending on the species, the smolt may spend up to two years in the stream before returning to the ocean.

The different species of salmon, and even sub-populations of the same species from separate streams, re-enter fresh water at different times – depending on water temperature and flows.

Generally, the best time to view coho and chum is in fall when they return to spawn in coastal streams that are rising from the autumn rains. Pink salmon is another coastal spawner, returning in summer.

American dipper

Sockeye return to rivers which have large lakes, typically entering freshwater in the summer months. Chinook or king salmon, the largest salmon species reaching over 22 kilograms/50 pounds, return in summer and fall.

Steelhead and sea-run coastal trout are close relatives and have similar life cycles to the salmon. However, unlike salmon, these fish survive after spawning to return again to the ocean.

A convenient way to view salmon close-up is to visit one of the many fish hatcheries found in British Columbia and Washington State.

Biodiversity

In many ways salmon represent the biodiversity of the Salish Sea. Many other wildlife species depend on salmon for food. Sea lions and seals congregate in fall at river mouths to intercept the returning fish. Bald eagles, gulls, mink, racoons, river otters and bears gorge on dead salmon each winter in the coastal rivers. Great blue herons feed on juvenile fish sheltering in estuaries in eelgrass beds. A small songbird, the American dipper, is found only in clear salmon streams with abundant

great blue heron

invertebrates and thus depends indirectly on nutrients released by decaying salmon.

The abundance and diversity of separate salmon stocks found in the different rivers and streams are indicators of environmental health. Salmon require clean, cold water and shaded, silt-free gravel beds. Dam building, poor logging practices, urban development, and agricultural and industrial pollution have reduced salmon populations.

coho salmon

River, Lake and Wetlands Route

Given the heavy winter rains, it should not be surprising that there are excellent examples of freshwater habitats around the Salish Sea. Superb examples are located just east of Vancouver along the north shore of the Fraser River. Here you can visit a number of different wetland, lake, forest and mountain habitats. The Fraser River is not only the world's most important salmon river, but is home to large sturgeon and many other species of fish. This route can be done as a day excursion from Vancouver.

red-winged blackbird

northern pintails

dragonfly

winter thaw at Oliphant Lake

Sitka burnet

Fresh Water Habitat

Different freshwater wetlands are distinguished by characteristic plants. Small trees and shrubs such as stream bank willows, Pacific crab apple, black hawthorn, snowberry and elderberry are associated with areas subject to flooding. If you see large black cottonwood trees, you are looking at a river floodplain subject to extensive flooding.

black hawthorn

Ponds or quiet lakes will have yellow water lilies and duckweed floating on the surface, and are edged with horse tail, sedges and hardhack. Cattails and tule grow in the quiet waters of marshes. Seeps, wet meadows and stream banks characteristically have marsh marigolds and other flowers from the buttercup family.

The nutrient poor, acidic and stagnant water of peat bogs is a special habitat characterized by sphagnum mosses. Extensive peat bogs were found in Richmond south of Vancouver. Much of this bog in the Fraser River lowlands has now been converted to cranberry farms. Less conspicuous are the small bogs found at all elevations throughout the Salish Sea. Growing in these habitats are specialized plants such as cranberry, round-leaved sundew, Sitka burnet and various orchids - and mosquitoes!

black cottonwood

Vancouver to Harrison Hot Springs

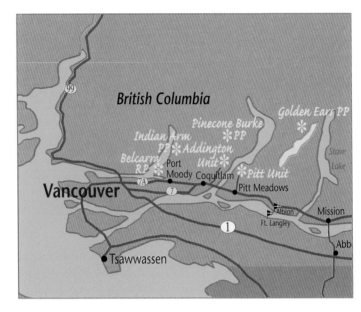

Take Hwy 7 *(Lougheed Highway)* along the north shore of the Fraser River from Vancouver to the vicinity of Coquitlam, 20 km/12 miles east of downtown. From here you can reach the Pitt-Addington Wildlife Management Area. An alternate route from Vancouver to the north shore of the Fraser River follows Hwy 7A to Port Moody. Along the way you can visit **Belcarra Regional Park** and **Indian Arm Provincial Park** which border a large salt water fiord.

North of Coquitlam is the undeveloped **Pinecone Burke Provincial Park**. It adjoins Pitt Lake and contains Widgeon Slough. Further east on Hwy 7 north of Pitt Meadows is **Golden Ears Provincial Park**. To reach Harrison Hot

coyote

Springs turn north onto Hwy 9 at Agassiz *(90 km/57 miles east of Coquitlam)*. Go east to Hope and the junction of Highways 1 and 5 or cross the Fraser River at Agassiz to return to Vancouver on Hwy 1.

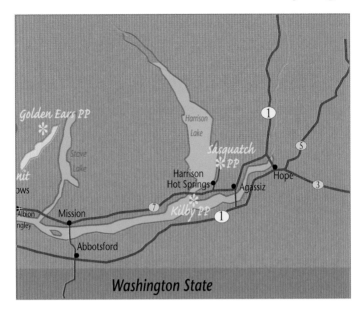

Pitt-Addington Wildlife Management Area

This is one of the largest waterfowl reserves in Canada. It consists of dyked wetlands, mudflats, riverside marshland and forested uplands. There are trails on the dikes and observation towers. More than 230 species of birds have been recorded. Sandhill cranes, great blue herons, green herons, harriers, ospreys and songbirds nest here. Bald eagles, trumpeter swans and many duck species overwinter. There are beaver, muskrat, black-tailed deer and black bear. On the west bank of the Pitt River just north of Port Coquitlam is the **Addington Marsh Unit**. To reach this site, leave Hwy 7 and go north on Coast Meridian Road. Turn left and follow Victoria Drive *(becoming Quarry Drive)* to **Minnekhada Regional Park**. Walk east from here, or north from Deboville Slough, to Addington Marsh. The **Pitt Unit**, on the east bank of the river, is 10 km/6 miles north from Pitt Meadows.

Vicinity of Harrison Hot Springs

Kilby Provincial Park is on the east bank of Harrison River just off Hwy 7, 13 km/8 miles west of Agassiz. Over a thousand bald eagles feed on chinook salmon from November to January. Trumpeter swans also overwinter here. On the edge of Harrison Lake past the Hot Springs resort are Hicks Lake and the marsh at **Sasquatch Provincial Park**.

cascara

pussy willows

red-winged blackbird

Pacific dogwood

junco

ladies' tresses orchid

painted turtle

Cooper's hawk

Lorquin's admiral

chocolate lily

ocean spray

Garry oak meadow

fawn lily

Urban Excursions

Seattle, Victoria and Vancouver offer excellent year-round wildlife viewing - by foot or by public transportation. You can make arrangements for bus tours or boat tours or guided

wilderness excursions from the city centres. These cities also have fine natural history museums or aquariums, with exhibits featuring the Salish Sea.

sea lion

belted kingfisher

Seattle

Bonaparte's gulls

Seattle - Bremerton Ferry

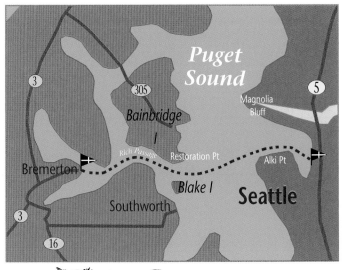

Seattle's greatest asset for the casual naturalist is easy access to the ferries and tour boats plying Puget Sound. One recommended trip is the 50 minute Washington State Ferry to Bremerton. Other attractions are the **Seattle Aquarium,** conveniently located at Pier 59, and the **Burke Museum of Natural History and Culture** on the University of Washington campus. From July through September you can view migrating salmon and sea lions at the **Lake Washington Ship Canal Fish Ladder**.

Buy a return ticket and board the ferry to Bremerton at Colmon Docks off downtown's historic Pioneer Square. Look for Alki Point to the south, 10 minutes after leaving the Seattle docks. For the next 15 minutes the ferry crosses the open waters of Puget Sound. After 20 minutes you will see Blake Island to the south. To the north is the low kelp-lined shore of Bainbridge Island's Restoration Point. Here the ferry winds through the strong currents of Rich Passage. Look for Bonaparte's gulls, scoters, loons and bald eagles as well as salmon pens. On a clear day there will be changing views of Mt. Rainier. The ferry then turns and continues southwest passing Manette Bridge *(connecting East Bremerton to Bremerton)* before docking beside the naval base.

In **Victoria**

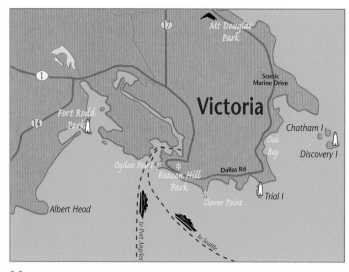

Victoria is ringed by the "sea-to-sea greenbelt", a large system of semi-wilderness parks which extends from the protected waters of Saanich Inlet to the Sooke Basin and the Strait of Juan de Fuca. Such a diversity of habitats offers countless opportunities to delight the naturalist. There are also excellent urban excursions, some of which are presented here. You might also consider a visit to the **Royal British Columbia Museum** for the natural history and First Nations' exhibits.

great blue heron in Beacon Hill Park

sweet peas

Beacon Hill Park and Dallas Road

Beacon Hill, a short walk from downtown Victoria and the harbour, has gulls and native spring wildflowers in camas meadows. There is excellent marine wildlife and bird viewing along the Dallas Road waterfront from the Ogden Point breakwater to Clover Point. You can see kelp

female mallard

beds, seals or possibly a river otter. In winter sea lions are common along the shore.

Oak Bay and Cattle Point

Take a scenic 10 minute drive along the waterfront from Clover Point, and you will reach Cattle Point on the rocky shore of Oak Bay. Close offshore are Greater Chain *(an ecological reserve)*, Trial and Discovery Islands. Because these are important nesting sites, pelagic cormorants, glaucous-winged gulls and pigeon guillemots are common even in summer. In fall and late winter there is an influx of grebes, harlequin ducks, black turnstones and sea lions. You can see bald eagles and even peregrine falcons here. In summer on occasion, you might be lucky enough to see an orca along the shore.

Mt. Douglas Park

Follow the Scenic Drive signs from downtown Victoria and Oak Bay to reach Mt. Douglas. Drive or hike through a Douglas-fir forest to reach the summit. You will have a panoramic view of the

Gulf and San Juan Islands, Mt. Baker and the Olympic Peninsula. In spring there are wildflowers among the Douglas-firs, madrone and stunted Garry oaks. Stonecrop and wild onions flower in early summer among the moss covered rocks.

flowering stonecrop

In and Around

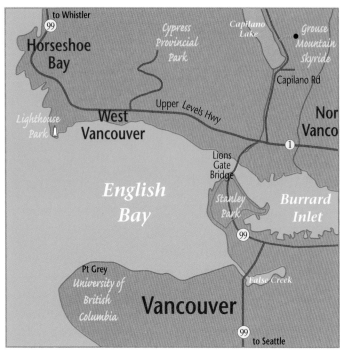

Considering the density of its urban development, Vancouver has a surprising number of accessible get-aways including some mountain areas of true wilderness. Two very interesting places you might consider visiting are described here.

Stanley Park

If you are in Vancouver for a short stay, this is the one excursion to make. This 500 ha/1,235 acre park, forested in Douglas-fir and western redcedar, can be reached from the downtown hotel zone by foot or city bus. You can walk around the park on the 8 km/5 mile car-free seawall which provides scenic views of the harbour, English

old growth western red cedar

Bay, and the North Shore mountains. You can also visit the nearby beaches. While there are birds to be seen in the park year-round, winter is special for the large flocks of seabirds and waterfowl. The **Vancouver Aquarium** is located here.

Vancouver

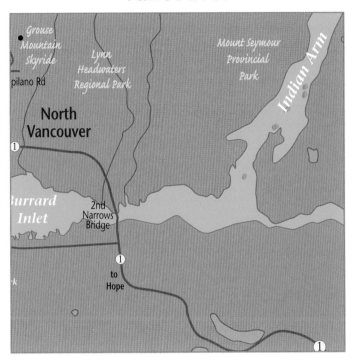

Grouse Mountain Skyride

Located on the North Shore mountains, this resort provides summer access via an aerial tramway to a 1,100 m/3,630 ft elevation. You can also take a chairlift to the 1,250 m/4,125 ft summit. As you rise above the redcedar and Douglas-fir, notice how the forest changes to mountain hemlock, amabilis fir and yellow-cedar. On the hiking paths, look for black-tailed deer, coyotes, bear, ravens, Steller's jays and whiskey jacks. There is a restaurant and exceptional views to the south of Vancouver, the San Juan and Gulf

Steller's jay

Islands and Mt. Baker. To reach Grouse Mountain from downtown, you go through Stanley Park and over the Lions Gate Bridge to the Upper Levels Highway, before turning east to Capilano Road. En route you might also visit the **Capilano Fish Hatchery**. There is also regular service by public transportation.

Trip Planning Info

FERRIES

BC Ferries	Victoria or out of Province	(250) 386-3431
	BC	1-888-223-3779
		www.bcferries.bc.ca
Washington State Ferries	Seattle or out of State	(206) 464-6400
	Washington State	1-800-843-3779
	BC	(250) 381-1551
		www.wsdot.wa.gov/ferries
Black Ball Ferries	Port Angeles	(360) 457-4491
	Victoria	(250) 386-2202
Victoria Rapid Transit	Port Angeles	(360) 452-8088
	Victoria	(250) 361-9144
	Washington State	1-800-633-1589
Clipper Navigation	Seattle	(206) 448-5000
	Victoria	(250) 382-8100
	Elsewhere	1-800-888-2535
Victoria-San Juan Cruises *(Bellingham to Victoria)*		1-800-443-4552
Alberni Marine Transportation Company *(Lady Rose)*		(250) 723-8313
		1-800-663-7192
Nootka Sound Services *(Uchuck II)*		(250) 283-2325

TOURIST BUREAUS

Tourism British Columbia   1-800-663-6000
Super Natural British Columbia   www.travel.bc.ca
Parliament Buildings
Victoria, BC V8V 1X4

Washington State Department of Tourism   1-800-544-1800
Olympia Headquarters   www.tourism.wa.gov
1114 Washington Street N.E.
P.O. Box 47000
Olympia, WA 98504

PARKS

Mt. Rainier National Park   (360) 569-2211
Ashford, WA 98304-9751   www.nps.gov/mora

Olympic National Park   (360) 452-0330
600 East Park Avenue   www.nps.gov/o
Port Angeles, WA 98362-6798

Washington State Parks and Recreation Headquarters
P.O. Box 42650
Olympia, WA 98504
     information   1-800-233-0321
     reservations   1-800-452-5687

Pacific Rim National Park Reserve   (250) 726-7721
P.O. Box 280   www.harbour.com/parkscan/pacrim
Ucluelet, BC V0R 3AO

BC Parks Headquarters
2nd Floor - 800 Johnson Street
Victoria, B.C. V8V 1X4   www.elp.gov.bc.ca/bcparks
     information   (250) 387-5002
     camping reservations   Vancouver   (604) 689-9025
                      elsewhere   1-800-689-9025

Photo Credits

photos used with permission; numbers refer to page; letters go left to right. top to bottom

Philip Critchlow: 7a,8b,71c,73b,84c,96b,98a,99a,114a,116a,128e

Derrick Ditchburn: Front Cover-great blue heron
45a,45e,50a,53a,54a,57e,58b,58f,61a,61b,63b,63c,64a,69a,69b,71b,74a,
87b,87f,89b,92b,92c,115b,124b,124c,126a,129b,135a

Nancy Dolan: Front Cover-madrone bark, satin flower, old growth
forest & shoreline
5a,6b,6d,10a,10c,11a,12a,17a,21c,25b,26a,27a,27b,27d,27e,33a,37a,38
a,45c,45d,46a,47b,47c,50b,50c,51a,52a,54b,57a,58c,62a,65b,67a,67b,
67c,67e,68a,72a,72c,73c,73d,73e,74b,75a,77b,78a,78b,78c,78d,79a,
79b,79c,79d,79f,79g,79i,79k,79l,79m,79n,79o,81b,82a,84a,85b,85c,86a
,86b,86c,86d,86e,86f,86g,87a,87c,87d,88a,89a,90a,91a,91b,91c,92a,93a
,93b,94a,94b,95a,95b,100a,100b,100c,100d,101a,102a,102b,103b,103c,
103d,104b,104c,105a,105b,105c,106a,107a,107b,107c,107d,108a,109a,
110a,110b,111a,112b,113a,113b,114b,114c,114d,115c,115d,117a,117b,
118a,118b,118c,119a,119b,120a,123b,124a,124d,128b,128d,129c,
129d,129f,132a,132b,133a,133b,134a

Jonathan Grant: 26c,34a,58a,74c,83b,95c

Marie O'Shaughnessy:
27c,57b,57d,63a,65a,66c,85a,97a,97c,104a,106b,122b,130e

Nicky Peck: 36a

Gary Schaan: Front Cover-blood sea star, Back Cover-Comox estuary
& ferry at Ogden Point
2a,6a,6c,10b,10d,15a,18a,18b,19a,20a,20b,21a,21b,22a,23a,24a,25a,
26b,29a,30a,31a,32a,39a,44a,45b,45f,46b,47a,50d,53b,55a,56a,56b,57c,
58d,58e,59a,59b,60a,60b,65c,66a,66b,66e,67d,69c,70a,71a,72b,73a,
75b,75c,76a,76b,77a,79e,79h,79j,80a,81a,83a,84b,89c,94c,96a,97b,
100e,103a,112a,115a,118d,122a,123a,124e,125a,125b,128a,128c,128f,
128g,129a,129e,130a,130b,130c,130d

British Columbia Archives: p40 (H6525), p41 (H04543),
p43 (F02584)

Line Drawings by Nancy Dolan

Maps by Nancy Dolan & Gary Schaan